READ THIS!

D0377647

Read this!

Handpicked Favorites from America's Indie Bookstores

COFFEE HOUSE PRESS
MINNEAPOLIS
2012

COFFEE HOUSE PRESS books are available to the trade through our primary distributor, Consortium Book Sales & Distribution, cbsd.com or (800) 283-3572. For personal orders, catalogs, or other information, write to: info@coffeehousepress.org.

Coffee House Press is a nonprofit literary publishing house. Support from private foundations, corporate giving programs, government programs, and generous individuals helps make the publication of our books possible. We gratefully acknowledge their support in detail in the back of this book. To you and our many readers around the world, we send our thanks for your continuing support.

Good books are brewing at coffeehousepress.org.

LIBRARY OF CONGRESS CIP INFORMATION
Read this! : handpicked favorites from
America's indie bookstores / edited
by Hans Weyandt ; introduction by Ann Patchett.
pages cm
Includes bibliographical references.
ISBN 978-1-56689-313-8 (alk. paper)
1. Best books.
2. Independent bookstores—Employees—Books and reading.
3. Books and reading—United States.
I. Weyandt, Hans.
Z1035.9.R43 2012
011'.73—DC23
2012008532
PRINTED IN THE UNITED STATES
1 3 5 7 9 8 6 4 2
FIRST EDITION | FIRST PRINTING

EDITOR'S ACKNOWLEDGMENTS

I need to thank David Unowsky for giving me my start at the Hungry Mind bookstore; thanks also to all the other booksellers (but especially Chris Hubbuch, Melanie Miller, and Carey Starr) for taking me under their wing. Thanks to my Micawber's cohorts Karen Reither and Tom Bielenberg (the other co-owner, who is quietly one of the top buyers in the country), who have been here since the beginning, and everyone else who has been here along the way. I need to give Liberty Hardy an extra shout for all of the enthusiasm and help she provided in making this endeavor zip and zoom all over the electronic book world.

I'm biased, of course, but the Twin Cities book world is as good as it gets. The sales reps, the people of all stripes who work for local publishers and distributors, the reviewers, and the booksellers here have my utmost love and respect.

Finally, I want to thank my parents for always having books around and making them part of our daily lives. And to Samuel, Elliott, and Jen: you make every day bigger, brighter, and better.

CONTENTS

Lists

BY ANN PATCHETT

Years ago, while cleaning out my desk (something I am prone to do during very long phone conversations), I found a crumpled yellow sticky note attached to the bottom of a drawer. The note read:

> *The Leopard,* Giuseppe di Lampedusa
> *The Radetzky March,* Joseph Roth
> *Her First American,* Lore Segal

It was in my own handwriting, but that doesn't matter. People are forever recommending books to me, and I am forever writing them down and putting the note someplace safe so I'll be sure to remember to buy them later. It doesn't always work. This particular list was startling because in the six months prior to its discovery, I had read *The Leopard* and *The Radetzky March.* They had come to me from two different people who had nothing to do with this note at all. I had loved both of the books madly. Madly! I had recently forced these exact two books on a neighbor who was heading off on vacation. Whoever told me to write down *The Leopard* and *The Radetzky March* was a person whose tastes I agreed with wholeheartedly. I had to assume that the third book on the list, *Her First American,* would be every bit as good.

And that was exactly the case. What a perfectly unique and memorable book Lore Segal wrote. I can close my eyes right this minute and am back in that dark New York hotel room with Ilka and Carter. Who was this person who had recommended the three best books I had read in ages? Who knew me well enough to know they were perfect for me? What else might he or she have recommended had there been more time or a second sticky note?

Not only do I take other people's recommendations for books to heart, I have been recommending them myself for as long as I've been reading. The desire to share books is the natural outcome of loving them, which is why working in a bookstore is such a pleasure. All day long people come in and ask me what they should read. And while it's great to hand over a hardback from the new release table, the deepest satisfaction comes from the asking and answering of questions—what did you love recently and what did you love the most? If you are exactly the right person, I'll bring you a copy of *Independent People* by Halldor Laxness. I understand that the number of people who can take on a 512-page novel about Iceland, sheep, and strong black coffee are few and far between, and that if I pressed it on everyone who came in the door we'd be out of business in no time, but this is a strange and brilliant novel, and if it's for you, it may well turn out to be one of your favorite books (as it is one of mine.) There is no greater joy for a bookseller than introducing a reader to a book they will love for the rest of their lives. Those of us in this business are, after all, matchmakers at heart.

So consider this little book you now hold in your hands a sort of catalogue of matchmakers. Not only do you get some background questions (Who do you trust to recommend books? What is on your nightstand right now?), you get thoughtful and extensive lists of favorites. I hadn't read all the books on any one person's list, but I could see whose taste mine aligned with and whose I didn't quite agree with. The lists that interested me the most were full of books I'd never heard of, because, after all, there was a time I had never heard of *The Leopard,* or *The Radetzky March,* or *Her First American.*

Bookselling is considered something of a risky business these days. People love to talk about how books are dead, and bookstores are dead. They say we are careening toward a world of electronic downloads and faceless internet ordering, to which I say, *Get thee to an independent bookstore.* We are alive and well, and we trust that you, the reader, will keep us that way. We can offer you something that other venues will never electronically reproduce: a conversation. After all, we know a lot of good books we'd like to introduce you to.

Preface

Bookselling is a career unlike many others. It isn't like becoming a doctor or lawyer or teacher, in which there is great prestige or a specific educational plan. I have yet to meet anyone who planned on becoming a career bookseller. It is a job most people fall into, and eventually fall in love with, when they get bitten by "the bug"—We pair a book with a particular person; they come back and tell us, "Yes, this book was a good fit for me." That simple reaction ignites something deep within us: a desire to keep pairing good people with good books.

Lately it's become en vogue to describe booksellers as "tastemakers" or "curators." While I'm not really sold on either term, it is true that booksellers are professional readers, among other things. Our job is to constantly search through the new and old to find works that entertain and challenge us, and make us want to pass them on. It is this desire, to share the fruits of our never-ending quest for great books with as many people as possible, that is at the heart of *Read This!*

ABOUT THIS BOOK

This entire endeavor has been filled with the spirit and power of kismet. A customer I had never met before asked me to name some of my top one hundred books. I mistakenly thought she meant my store's one hundred *best-selling* titles. When she corrected me, saying she was looking for some of my personal favorites, my mind began to churn. This was a fun and bewildering and tough and amazing task—I'd never thought of books I loved in terms of a top ten, fifty, or one hundred. After I sold her some of my favorites, I began to think of her question in larger terms. How would a list I made compare to those of my comrades in the bookselling world? What if we could create a master list from people in bookstores across the country? What kind of odd database might we build?

I began calling and e-mailing colleagues with a simple request: name fifty books you love or love to pass on to other readers. The responses were immediate and surprising in wonderful ways. As I made my way from person to person, I found they were eager to share the books they loved to hand sell. At the end of each conversation I asked for another recommendation—what bookseller should I speak to next? A network of like-minded souls quickly began to form. All the differences between us—our ages, our regions and states, our genders and appearances—were quickly minimized by our mutual commitment to books.

All too often we booksellers are asked about the negative parts of this business—and there are many. We're asked to prognosticate about a future that is very much up in the air. We're asked about the closings of other bookstores, small and large. This project was remarkable because it was entirely focused on the positives and what we all ultimately love about our jobs: the books.

Keep in mind, these lists represent a moment in time. Without minimizing the importance of the particular books chosen here, these lists are not written in stone. Many of us could do endless variations of our lists. We all have mental catalogues of odd books and funny novels and moving memoirs, or editions of poetry and cookbooks.

Proceeds from this book will go to the American Booksellers Foundation for Free Expression (www.abffe.org). It is a group that constantly and tirelessly works in the background to support what independent booksellers work for. They fight against the banning of books and provide support for stores that run into trouble by providing access to information and content. We're happy to give back to them in whatever way we can.

—H. W.

READ THIS!

Micawber's Books

ST. PAUL, MN

Operating since 1972 in St. Paul, Minnesota, Micawber's Books was voted best bookstore in the Twin Cities for new books by *City Pages* in 2007 and 2010. In a small and cozy space, Micawber's sells books from local authors and publishers and is also well stocked in general fiction, nonfiction, and poetry. Browsers can find hand-written endorsements on index cards taped to shelves around the store.

www.micawbers.com

Who is your most trusted source for book recommendations?
It's an unfortunate aspect of being a bookseller, but very few people tell me what to read. I do have a rule that forces me to read any book that three customers recommend. Johanna Hynes and Steve Horwitz are two of our sales reps who I feel really get my taste and always show me to the right books or challenge me with things I otherwise wouldn't look at.

What is your favorite bookstore (besides the one you work at)?
Three Lives, in New York City, is my personal book heaven. It's a small space but not a small inventory. When I browse there, I feel like every single book has been hand selected. I always find new and old things I didn't know about and feel the need to read. The staff is helpful but not overbearing. Anytime someone tells me they're going to New York City, I write out directions to this wonderful space that can be tricky to find.

What is one thing about bookselling most people don't know?
It's a combo platter of bartender/barista and priest. We get to know customers in ways beyond what any electronic algorithm can provide. I've seen first dates and proposals.

We've hosted birthday parties and baby showers. Kids who waited for the new Harry Potter on hot August nights now drive by in cars. We get to interact with a community, and every single day is different and interesting.

What would be book number 51 on your list?

I recently read Stig Dagerman's *German Autumn,* which was published by the University of Minnesota Press. First published in 1947, it is an outsider's look at Germany after the fall of the Reich and wwii. It is journalism at its finest, with lucid prose that forced me to think of that time period and the German people in more complex ways than I ever had before. Like books on Bob Dylan and Abraham Lincoln, there is no shortage of wwii stuff out there, but this belongs in the very top tier.

- [ ] **A Universal History of the Destruction of Books: From Ancient Sumer to Modern-Day Iraq,** Fernando Báez
- [ ] **The Ninemile Wolves,** Rick Bass
- [ ] **You Can't Win,** Jack Black
- [ ] **Postville: A Clash of Cultures in Heartland America,** Stephen G. Bloom
- [ ] **On the Yard,** Malcolm Braly
- [ ] **Running After Antelope,** Scott Carrier
- [ ] **My Ántonia,** Willa Cather
- [ ] **George and Rue,** George Elliott Clarke
- [ ] **Open City,** Teju Cole
- [ ] **Newjack: Guarding Sing Sing,** Ted Conover
- [ ] **The Brothers K,** David James Duncan
- [ ] **Geek Love,** Katherine Dunn
- [ ] **The Farther Shore,** Matthew Eck
- [ ] **The Solace of Open Spaces,** Gretel Ehrlich
- [ ] **Every Man Dies Alone,** Hans Fallada
- [ ] **Going Blind,** Mara Faulkner, OSB
- [ ] **Bury Me Standing: The Gypsies and Their Journey,** Isabel Fonseca
- [ ] **Hell at the Breech,** Tom Franklin

- [ ] **Great Plains,** Ian Frazier
- [ ] **The Last American Man,** Elizabeth Gilbert
- [ ] **We Wish to Inform You That Tomorrow We Will Be Killed with Our Families: Stories from Rwanda,** Philip Gourevitch
- [ ] **A Writer at War: Vasily Grossman with the Red Army, 1941–1945,** Vasily Grossman
- [ ] **Reasons to Live,** Amy Hempel
- [ ] **What the Living Do,** Marie Howe
- [ ] **Seek: Reports from the Edges of America & Beyond,** Denis Johnson
- [ ] **A Walker in the City,** Alfred Kazin
- [ ] **Garden, Ashes,** Danilo Kis
- [ ] **Miniatures,** Norah Labiner
- [ ] **The Boat,** Nam Le
- [ ] **With Borges,** Alberto Manguel
- [ ] **So Long, See You Tomorrow,** William Maxwell
- [ ] **Letter to an Imaginary Friend,** Thomas McGrath
- [ ] **The Headmaster,** John McPhee
- [ ] **Up in the Old Hotel,** Joseph Mitchell
- [ ] **All the Living,** C. E. Morgan
- [ ] **The Things They Carried,** Tim O'Brien
- [ ] **Mystery and Manners: Occasional Prose,** Flannery O'Connor

- [ ] **In the Skin of a Lion,** Michael Ondaatje
- [ ] **The Time of Our Singing,** Richard Powers
- [ ] **Down in My Heart,** William Stafford
- [ ] **Jesse James: Last Rebel of the Civil War,** T. J. Stiles
- [ ] **The Gangster We Are All Looking For,** lê thi diem thúy
- [ ] **The Tummy Trilogy,** Calvin Trillin
- [ ] **Maps of the Imagination: The Writer as Cartographer,** Peter Turchi
- [ ] **The Tiger: A True Story of Vengeance and Survival,** John Vaillant
- [ ] **The Book of Fathers,** Miklós Vámos
- [ ] **A Book of Reasons,** John Vernon
- [ ] **Lone Wolf: Eric Rudolph and the Legacy of American Terror,** Maryanne Vollers
- [ ] **Essays of E. B. White**
- [ ] **In the American Grain,** William Carlos Williams

Reasons to Live, Amy Hempel

This selection was difficult because I love all of her books nearly equally and often feel the need to defend the short story from unjust persecution. While I tend to like longer short stories, Hempel brings such emotion and depth to her short work that I can never decide on a favorite story or line. Every time I read her there is a new lightbulb moment or punch to the heart.

Miniatures, Norah Labiner

I consider it a personal obligation to the world of fiction readers to talk about Norah Labiner's *Miniatures* any chance I get a forum to recommend books. It's a novel about fame, art, storytelling, and culture (both high and pop). She tells, retells, lists. The book is frenetic. It is a maze. It spirals around itself. I truly believe that Labiner is a wordsmith of the highest order.

Letter to an Imaginary Friend, Thomas McGrath

To me, this book is as much an American masterpiece as jazz or baseball. Written over more than twenty-five years and first published in its entirety in 1997 by Copper Canyon Press, this book is a mash-up in form and tone and voice. The fact that it isn't more widely read and con-sidered one of our finer epic works is a shame.

Jesse James: Last Rebel of the Civil War, T. J. Stiles

This biography is an important work because it does not, as most other historical James accounts tend to do, make him a simple redneck outlaw or Robin Hood–esque hero. The times and area he lived in were full of philosophical gray areas and shape-shifting boundaries. I grew up hearing stories about the James Gang, and many of the areas he frequented are portions of the United States that I know well.

Book Passage

CORTE MADERA, CA

Book Passage opened in 1976, with stores in Marin County and San Francisco's Ferry Building. Book Passage averages more than seven hundred author events per year for people of all ages and interest. Many of these events are also benefits for local charitable organizations.

Book Passage offers a program of in-store classes about writing, language learning, and the book business. They also host three annual writing conferences for mystery writers; children's writers and illustrators; and a travel, food, and photography conference. Book Passage hosts book groups in-store and also sells used books on behalf of Hospice by the Bay.

www.bookpassage.com

SHERYL COTLEUR, HEAD BUYER

Who is your most trusted source for book recommendations?
Fellow buyers especially, such as Paul Yamazaki at City Lights, Cathy Langer at Tattered Cover, Rick Simonson at Elliott Bay, and Kevin Ryan at Green Apple, to name a few. And editors—not only their own books, but when they read something they love it's usually very worthy.

What makes a bookstore successful in today's world?
Curatorial care in choosing books, and enthusiastic plus thoughtful recommendations by staff—both between staff and from staff to customers. Basically just great conversation about books.

What is one thing about bookselling most people don't know?
How much hard work it is to stay on top of the ebb and flow of inventory, cash flow, late-breaking news, and all the myriad events that affect what you want to have and when and how many copies. It's exhilarating but also hard work.

What book is on your nightstand right now?
Five Bells, by Gail Jones. It's awesome!

What is your favorite bookstore (besides the one you work at)?
City Lights is lots of fun to browse in, as their inventory is so very unusual.

- ☐ **Eva Luna,** Isabel Allende
- ☐ **On Canaan's Side,** Sebastian Barry
- ☐ **The Boys of My Youth,** Jo Ann Beard
- ☐ **Watch With Me,** Wendell Berry
- ☐ **The Widow and the Tree,** Sonny Brewer
- ☐ **The Tree of Meaning: Language, Mind and Ecology,** Robert Bringhurst
- ☐ **A Dry White Season,** André Brink
- ☐ **The Other Side of Eden: Hunters, Farmers, and the Shaping of the World,** Hugh Brody
- ☐ **Light at the Edge of the World: A Journey through the Realm of Vanishing Cultures,** Wade Davis
- ☐ **Classics for Pleasure,** Michael Dirda
- ☐ **The Gift of Rain,** Tan Twan Eng
- ☐ **Bear,** Marian Engel
- ☐ **We Wish to Inform You That Tomorrow We Will Be Killed with Our Families: Stories from Rwanda,** Philip Gourevitch
- ☐ **Tinkers,** Paul Harding
- ☐ **Power,** Linda Hogan

- [ ] **Bridge of Birds: A Novel of an Ancient China That Never Was,** Barry Hughart

- [ ] **Geography of the Heart,** Fenton Johnson

- [ ] **Mister Pip,** Lloyd Jones

- [ ] **Memories, Dreams, Reflections,** by C. G. Jung

- [ ] **The Wisdom of the Mythtellers,** Sean Kane

- [ ] **Kim,** Rudyard Kipling

- [ ] **Radical Hope: Ethics in the Face of Cultural Devastation,** Jonathan Lear

- [ ] **Move Your Shadow: South Africa, Black and White,** Joseph Lelyveld

- [ ] **The Storyteller,** Mario Vargas Llosa

- [ ] **Matterhorn: A Novel of the Vietnam War,** Karl Marlantes

- [ ] **At Play in the Fields of the Lord,** Peter Matthiessen

- [ ] **The Ancient Child,** N. Scott Momaday

- [ ] **Song of Solomon,** Toni Morrison (actually, everything by her)

- [ ] **Alive Together,** Lisel Mueller

- [ ] **Black Elk Speaks: Being the Life Story of a Holy Man of the Oglala Sioux,** John Neihardt

- [ ] **Twenty Poems of Love and a Song of Despair,** Pablo Neruda

- [ ] **The Tiger's Wife,** Téa Obreht

- [ ] **New and Selected Poems,** Mary Oliver
- [ ] **Running in the Family,** Michael Ondaatje
- [ ] **The Skull Mantra,** Eliot Pattison
- [ ] **The Grass Dancer,** Susan Power
- [ ] **Generosity: An Enhancement,** Richard Powers
- [ ] **Housekeeping,** Marilynne Robinson
- [ ] **An Ordinary Man,** Paul Rusesabagina
- [ ] **The Best of It,** Kay Ryan
- [ ] **Eye of the Albatross: Visions of Hope and Survival,** Carl Safina
- [ ] **Where Rivers Change Direction,** Mark Spragg
- [ ] **The People of the Sea: A Journey in Search of the Seal Legend,** David Thomson
- [ ] **The Lord of the Rings,** J. R. R. Tolkien
- [ ] **A Mantis Carol,** Laurens Van Der Post
- [ ] **La Maravilla,** Alfredo Véa, Jr.
- [ ] **The Man Who Killed the Deer: A Novel of Pueblo Indian Life,** Frank Waters
- [ ] **Lightning Bird: The Story of One Man's Journey into Africa's Past,** Lyall Watson
- [ ] **Refuge: An Unnatural History of Family and Place,** Terry Tempest Williams

Move Your Shadow: South Africa, Black and White,
Joseph Lelyveld
This Pulitzer Prize–winning book about life in South Africa under apartheid forever changed my life with its power and deeply moving stories, so much so that even twenty-five years later I cannot forget them.

Matterhorn: A Novel of the Vietnam War, Karl Marlantes
Such a powerful and well-told novel of a young Marine in combat in Vietnam; it deserves to be read by everyone.

The Ancient Child, N. Scott Momaday
Perhaps not as well known as his Pulitzer-winning *House Made of Dawn,* but absolutely poetic and brilliant. It's about an artist losing then finding himself—mixed with visits to Billy the Kid.

Where Rivers Change Direction, Mark Spragg
One of the best coming-of-age memoirs I've ever discovered of a young boy raised in Wyoming and coming into manhood and becoming a writer.

The People of the Sea: A Journey in Search of the Seal Legend, David Thomson
This is about the most charming yet informative book about Ireland just at the cusp (in the fifties) of being modernized—therefore still full of local color from the old stories told by those who still remember.

BookCourt

BookCourt has been a mainstay in Cobble Hill, Brooklyn, since 1981 and remains a family-run business to this day. BookCourt stocks mainly literary fiction and nonfiction, but one area of the store is devoted to local interests, including everything from guidebooks for weekend excursions to literary works about New York City. They also have a large room for children's books, offering a selection of both new and classic titles. The store is devoted to university and small press books, and loves to champion its many local authors. BookCourt hosts readings and events almost every night of the week, and is now open 365 days a year.

www.bookcourt.com

Who is your most trusted source for book recommendations?
There are reviewers I trust, and friends I trust, and book-sellers I trust. Really, my problem is that I have too many smart people recommending books to me all the time. My backlog is so enormous that often by the time I actually read a book, I've forgotten who told me they loved it or which newspaper gave it a rave. Then it's just up to me and the book to see if we can get along.

What book is on your nightstand right now?
I have a short stack of books on my nightstand: Kevin Wilson's *The Family Fang;* Alan Hollinghurst's *The Line of Beauty;* George Eliot's *Middlemarch,* which I'm reading for the fourth time, I think; the new issue of *The Paris Review;* and just to the left of my nightstand is my "to be read" bookshelf, which has about fifty books on it. So in a way, those books are on my nightstand too. Just imagine it's a very, very big nightstand.

What is your favorite bookstore (besides the one you work at)?
There are so many! I love Word, in Brooklyn, and Skylight and BookSoup in Los Angeles, and Elliott Bay in Seattle, and Powell's in Portland, just to name a few. I've been lucky enough to read at independent bookstores

across the country, and they are all unique and smart and wonderful. Whenever I'm in a new city, the first place I go is a bookstore. The only drawback to this plan is a very heavy suitcase.

EMMA'S LIST

- [ ] **Emma,** Jane Austen
- [ ] **Down the Street,** Lynda Barry
- [ ] **I Remember,** Joe Brainard
- [ ] **Wuthering Heights,** Emily Brontë
- [ ] **In Cold Blood,** Truman Capote
- [ ] **True History of the Kelly Gang,** Peter Carey
- [ ] **Where I'm Calling From,** Raymond Carver
- [ ] **The Amazing Adventures of Kavalier & Clay,** Michael Chabon
- [ ] **You Remind Me of Me,** Dan Chaon
- [ ] **The Great Man,** Kate Christensen
- [ ] **Everything Matters!,** Ron Currie Jr.
- [ ] **Bad Marie,** Marcy Dermansky
- [ ] **The Complete Poems of Emily Dickinson**
- [ ] **Entertaining is Fun: How to Be a Popular Hostess,** Dorothy Draper
- [ ] **Rebecca,** Daphne Du Maurier
- [ ] **A Visit from the Goon Squad,** Jennifer Egan
- [ ] **The Stories (So Far) of Deborah Eisenberg**
- [ ] **Middlemarch,** George Eliot
- [ ] **The Good Solider,** Ford Madox Ford

- [ ] **The Cost of Living: Early and Uncollected Stories,** Mavis Gallant
- [ ] **Philippe Halsman's Jump Book**
- [ ] **A Moveable Feast,** Ernest Hemingway
- [ ] **Never Let Me Go,** Kazuo Ishiguro
- [ ] **The Portrait of a Lady,** Henry James
- [ ] **New Addresses,** Kenneth Koch
- [ ] **Under the Banner of Heaven: A Story of Violent Faith,** Jon Krakauer
- [ ] **Unaccustomed Earth,** Jhumpa Lahiri
- [ ] **Random Family: Love, Drugs, Trouble, and Coming of Age in the Bronx,** Adrian Nicole LeBlanc
- [ ] **Magic for Beginners,** Kelly Link
- [ ] **George and Martha,** James Marshall
- [ ] **Liars and Saints,** Maile Meloy
- [ ] **Martin Dressler: The Tale of an American Dreamer,** Stephen Millhauser
- [ ] **Like Life,** Lorrie Moore
- [ ] **Chocolates for Breakfast,** Pamela Moore
- [ ] **Skippy Dies,** Paul Murray
- [ ] **Lolita,** Vladimir Nabokov
- [ ] **Lunch Poems,** Frank O'Hara
- [ ] **Bel Canto,** Ann Patchett
- [ ] **Little Children,** Tom Perrotta

- [ ] **Dress Your Family in Corduroy and Denim,** David Sedaris
- [ ] **Ideas of Heaven: A Ring of Stories,** Joan Silber
- [ ] **Memento Mori,** Muriel Spark
- [ ] **Crossing to Safety,** Wallace Stegner
- [ ] **Mystery,** Peter Straub
- [ ] **The Secret History,** Donna Tartt
- [ ] **The Master,** Colm Toibin
- [ ] **The Age of Innocence,** Edith Wharton
- [ ] **Stoner,** John Williams
- [ ] **Old School,** Tobias Wolff
- [ ] **The Wife,** Meg Wolitzer

Everything Matters!, Ron Currie Jr.
What if you were born with the exact knowledge of when a giant asteroid would hit the earth? This novel is inventive and wild, yes, but it's also heartfelt and genuinely human. I wept openly, in public.

Martin Dressler: The Tale of an American Dreamer,
Stephen Millhauser
Some novels loom so large in my memory that I can hardly believe they're novels, and not myths that have lasted thousands of years. This story of one man's life—his ambitions and loves and disappointments—is one of those books, set against the backdrop of a New York City hotel.

Chocolates for Breakfast, Pamela Moore
This fabulous novel has been out of print for ages but will be reissued by Harper Perennial in the near future, and I am beyond excited to be able to sell it. Imagine a sexier version of *The Bell Jar,* in Manhattan and Los Angeles. You see? You want to read it already.

The Wife, Meg Wolitzer
This novel is so sharp and funny, and is especially important reading for aspiring writers and those who love them. Wolitzer manages to pack an entire marriage's worth of resentment and pent-up feelings into this slim little book, and I wolfed it down all in one sitting.

Boswell Book Company

MILWAUKEE, WI

In April 2009, Boswell Book Company opened in the former location of the Downer Avenue Schwartz branch. Boswell is owned by Daniel Goldin, a twenty-three-year Schwartz veteran, and staffed by a spectrum of Milwaukee's best booksellers. They host several hundred authors each year and sell books at events in and around the larger community.

They can be found online at www.boswellbooks.com, and on Facebook and Twitter.

STACIE M. WILLIAMS, BOOKSELLER

What book first started your reading obsession?

More than any single title, the true inspiration behind my reading obsession is more apt to be the result of simple chemistry: a combination of nature and nurture. I was lucky enough to be born with a brain made for reading, followed by relentless encouragement from a reader/writer mother.

Certainly there were a few books that built the foundation for my house of turning pages: When I was seven, my mom read Dickens out loud to us at bedtime, specifically *Great Expectations* and *A Tale of Two Cities*. Then, a fourth-grade talent show audition had me memorizing Shakespeare. And finally, when I was twelve, I plucked Margaret Atwood's *The Handmaid's Tale* off a shelf. However, I was slightly derailed when Mom caught me reading it in church and told me I wasn't yet old enough and had to wait a few more years. When I did eventually read it, I was hooked. My junior year of high school, I used it for an honors English thesis consisting of five themed essays, clinching Atwood as my writing idol, though her 1988 novel *Cat's Eye* ultimately became my favorite of her works.

And so the list began.

- ☐ **The Hitchhiker's Guide to the Galaxy,** Douglas Adams
- ☐ **Watership Down,** Richard Adams
- ☐ **The Yacoubian Building,** Alaa Al Aswany
- ☐ **Brothel: Mustang Ranch and Its Women,** Alexa Albert
- ☐ **Canine Body Language: A Photographic Guide Interpreting the Native Language of the Domestic Dog,** Brenda Aloff
- ☐ **Wake Up, Sir!,** Jonathan Ames
- ☐ **Cat's Eye,** Margaret Atwood
- ☐ **Deer Hunting with Jesus: Dispatches from America's Class War,** Joe Bageant
- ☐ **Willful Creatures,** Aimee Bender
- ☐ **Things That Fall from the Sky,** Kevin Brockmeier
- ☐ **Nine Parts of Desire: The Hidden World of Islamic Women,** Geraldine Brooks
- ☐ **Numbers in the Dark: And Other Stories,** Italo Calvino
- ☐ **Five Skies,** Ron Carlson
- ☐ **When Things Fall Apart: Heart Advice for Difficult Times,** Pema Chodron
- ☐ **The Awakening,** Kate Chopin
- ☐ **Selected Poems, 1945–2005,** Robert Creeley
- ☐ **The Art of Living,** Epictetus

- [ ] **Don't Sleep, There Are Snakes: Life and Language in the Amazonian Jungle,** Daniel Everett
- [ ] **The Tsar's Dwarf,** Peter H. Fogtdal
- [ ] **A Passage to India,** E. M. Forster
- [ ] **Smonk,** Tom Franklin
- [ ] **I Hate to See That Evening Sun Go Down,** William Gay
- [ ] **Tales of a Female Nomad: Living at Large in the World,** Rita Golden Gelman
- [ ] **Ghosts of Wyoming,** Alyson Hagy
- [ ] **The Best Day the Worst Day: Life with Jane Kenyon,** Donald Hall
- [ ] **Daughters of the North,** Sarah Hall
- [ ] **Mariette in Ecstasy,** Ron Hansen
- [ ] **Blue Latitudes: Boldly Going Where Captain Cook Has Gone Before,** Tony Horwitz
- [ ] **The Attack,** Yasmina Khadra
- [ ] **Pack of Two: The Intricate Bond Between People and Dogs,** Caroline Knapp
- [ ] **Under the Banner of Heaven: A Story of Violent Faith,** Jon Krakauer
- [ ] **When I Was Mortal,** Javier Marías
- [ ] **Outer Dark,** Cormac McCarthy
- [ ] **Savage Beauty: The Life of Edna St. Vincent Millay,** Nancy Milford

- [ ] **Lipstick Jihad: A Memoir of Growing Up Iranian in America and American in Iran,** Azadeh Moaveni
- [ ] **The Lust Lizard of Melancholy Cove,** Christopher Moore
- [ ] **Arturo's Island,** Elsa Morante
- [ ] **Senselessness,** Horacio Castellanos Moya
- [ ] **Mystery and Manners: Occasional Prose,** Flannery O'Connor
- [ ] **Coal Black Horse,** Robert Olmstead
- [ ] **The Dogs of Babel,** Carolyn Parkhurst
- [ ] **Out Stealing Horses,** Per Petterson
- [ ] **Serena,** Ron Rash
- [ ] **The Rapture of Canaan,** Sheri Reynolds
- [ ] **Arcadia,** Tom Stoppard
- [ ] **Darkness Visible: A Memoir of Madness,** William Styron
- [ ] **The Killer Inside Me,** Jim Thompson
- [ ] **How Fiction Works,** James Wood
- [ ] **Collected Letters by Elizabeth Bishop, Flannery O'Connor, T. S. Eliot, Yeats, Keats, Welty, Hemingway, Fitzgerald, pretty much anyone**

The Hitchhiker's Guide to the Galaxy, Douglas Adams
Nine Parts of Desire: The Hidden World of Islamic Women, Geraldine Brooks
The Awakening, Kate Chopin
The Art of Living, Epictetus
I Hate to See That Evening Sun Go Down, William Gay
Arcadia, Tom Stoppard

There are a few things I crave in life: knowledge, philosophy, connection, aesthetic experience, and just plain fun. These books each had an immense impact—a pendulum shift, of sorts—on my ways of thinking, feeling, seeing, or reading the world. When a young teen, I listened to the audio version of *THHGTTG,* read by Douglas Adams. A book had yet to make me laugh so hard. I even memorized the opening chapter to perform for a high school drama class audition (Yes, I'm that big of a nerd). Geraldine Brooks's narrative journey into the lives of the veiled and unveiled women of Islam opened my eyes to new cultures and faith, and spawned an unceasing interest in that world. The tiny, powerful novella that is Kate Chopin's most well-known work was assigned to me in high school and resonated deeply as a woman with instincts that reached beyond potential motherhood and into artistry. Epictetus taught me about letting go, reevaluating fear, and life too well lived. William Gay, oh William Gay; what can I say about this late-in-life author who looks into the darkest crevices of mankind and seeks out true souls with fiction, music, and paintings? Gone too soon. Language and science took on a whole new sheen and depth when I saw (and then read) Tom Stoppard's brilliant play, *Arcadia*. Of course, I could do this for each book on the list: that's the bookseller's curse.

Carmichael's Bookstore

LOUISVILLE, KY

Carmichael's Bookstore has been a family-run business since its opening in 1978. With two small retail sites, they offer a handpicked selection of titles reflecting the taste of the owners and the neighborhoods where they are located. They have an extensive collection of books of local interest, as well as a school division.

From its beginning, Carmichael's has been committed to being a neighborhood gathering place and is open seven days a week and every evening. Both stores are on corners in vibrant urban areas, "lively streetscapes never darkened by the shadow of a big box store." Carmichael's is a founding member of the Louisville Independent Business Alliance. They are committed to "keeping Louisville weird" and spreading the word about shopping local.

www.carmichaelsbookstore.com

MICHAEL BOGGS, CO-OWNER

What book is on your nightstand right now?
Adam Johnson's *The Orphan Master's Son,* Toby Lester's
Da Vinci's Ghost, Adam Gopnik's *The Table Comes First,*
and Richard Hoagland's *Sex and the River Styx.*

**Which book on your list do you think is particularly
underrated?**
Stone Virgin, Hair of Harold Roux, and *Any Human Heart.*

Who is your most trusted source for book recommendations?
Excerpts in the *New Yorker.*

What makes a bookstore successful in today's world?
A pathological aversion to political and cultural bland-
ness.

**What is your favorite bookstore (besides the one you
work at)?**
Bookshop Santa Cruz.

- ☐ **Lives of the Monster Dogs,** Kirsten Bakis
- ☐ **Rising Tide: The Great Mississippi Flood of 1927 and How it Changed America,** John M. Barry
- ☐ **Citizenship Papers,** Wendell Berry
- ☐ **The Way of Ignorance: And Other Essays,** Wendell Berry
- ☐ **Any Human Heart,** William Boyd
- ☐ **At Home: A Short History of Private Life,** Bill Bryson
- ☐ **A Walk in the Woods: Rediscovering America on the Appalachian Trail,** Bill Bryson
- ☐ **The Years of Lyndon Johnson, Vol. 1: The Path to Power,** Robert Caro
- ☐ **Little Bee,** Chris Cleave
- ☐ **The Hours,** Michael Cunningham
- ☐ **Underworld,** Don DeLillo
- ☐ **The White Album,** Joan Didion
- ☐ **Pilgrim at Tinker Creek,** Annie Dillard
- ☐ **The Spies of Warsaw,** Alan Furst
- ☐ **Sophie's World: A Novel About the History of Philosophy,** Jostein Gaarder
- ☐ **Neuromancer,** William Gibson
- ☐ **Paris to the Moon,** Adam Gopnik

- [ ] **The Curious Incident of the Dog in the Night-Time,** Mark Haddon
- [ ] **A Winter's Tale,** Mark Helprin
- [ ] **Dispatches,** Michael Herr
- [ ] **World According to Garp,** John Irving
- [ ] **The Stand,** Stephen King
- [ ] **Into the Wild,** Jon Krakauer
- [ ] **The Little Drummer Girl,** John Le Carré
- [ ] **Smiley's People,** John Le Carré
- [ ] **Atonement,** Ian McEwan
- [ ] **Lonesome Dove,** Larry McMurtry
- [ ] **The River of Doubt: Theodore Roosevelt's Darkest Journey,** Candice Millard
- [ ] **The Things They Carried,** Tim O'Brien
- [ ] **The English Patient,** Michael Ondaatje
- [ ] **The Orchid Thief: A True Story of Beauty and Obsession,** Susan Orlean
- [ ] **Metzger's Dog,** Thomas Perry
- [ ] **The Omnivore's Dilemma: A Natural History of Four Meals,** Michael Pollan
- [ ] **The Dog of the South,** Charles Portis
- [ ] **The Hot Zone: A Terrifying True Story,** Richard Preston
- [ ] **The Shipping News,** Annie Proulx
- [ ] **The Plot Against America,** Philip Roth

- [ ] **The Man Who Mistook His Wife for a Hat: And Other Clinical Tales,** Oliver Sacks
- [ ] **Me Talk Pretty One Day,** David Sedaris
- [ ] **Gorky Park,** Martin Cruz Smith
- [ ] **Snow Crash,** Neal Stephenson
- [ ] **The Secret History,** Donna Tartt
- [ ] **The Lives of a Cell: Notes of a Biology Watcher,** Lewis Thomas
- [ ] **Chinaman's Chance,** Ross Thomas
- [ ] **A Confederacy of Dunces,** John Kennedy Toole
- [ ] **The Guns of the South,** Harry Turtledove
- [ ] **Stone Virgin,** Barry Unsworth
- [ ] **The Hair of Harold Roux,** Thomas Williams
- [ ] **The Professor and the Madman: A Tale of Murder, Insanity, and the Making of the Oxford English Dictionary,** Simon Winchester

Citizenship Papers and **The Way of Ignorance and Other Essays,** Wendell Berry

Wendell Berry is Kentucky's literary treasure—poet, essayist, novelist, activist—a prolific and profound writer on the value and values of community, home, land, and family. My personal preference is for Berry's essays: seldom do you get powerful philosophical and political ideas shaped by the hands of a poet. These two collections are representative of a terrific writer who inspires you to not only think but to act.

Any Human Heart, William Boyd

Here we have the eighty-five-year life of one Logan Mountstuart, as narrated through journal entries spanning six decades. It's the kind of literary novel seldom written anymore—the story of an adult male who is reflective, charming, flawed, often beloved, and occasionally despicable. Mountstuart has triumphs, moving through the most elegant art salons of New York and Paris, and terrible reversals that leave him living in an unheated basement room in London. Through it all he demonstrates an unwavering love of life and an unflinching, honest appraisal of his own failures and accomplishments. The title comes from a wonderful quote from

Henry James—"Never say you know the last word about any human heart"—but William Boyd, with a deft empathy and lovely prose, does as much as one writer can do to uncover that last word.

Stone Virgin, Barry Unsworth

Despite winning the Booker prize for *Sacred Hunger,* Unsworth has never found a wide audience, especially in America. *Stone Virgin,* however, placed in the right reader's hands, is a very commercial novel from a highly literary writer. The main character is restoring a magnificent sixteenth-century statue of a Madonna, and as we trace four centuries of the statue's history, we discover the sinister journey that has left it neglected in an outdoor plaza in Venice. But there is some dark business afoot in the present as well, and *Stone Virgin* is charged with the psychological suspense of a modern thriller.

City Lights

SAN FRANCISCO, CA

Lawrence (Ferlinghetti) has always thought of City Lights as part of a long tradition of resistance and dissent, a beacon of possibility, and a place of refuge for considering the long horizon of possible futures. Lawrence felt it was imperative that City Lights be a place of lively stillness, where the browser/reader could peruse the shelves, select several books, and read them at her or his own pace.

Within the broad banks of resistance and possibility lie the foundations of City Lights's curatorial parameters, which, broadly stated, include making space for work that incites imagination and creative dissent. These curatorial parameters have been established over decades of thought, discussion, and practice among the staff of City Lights. All fourteen members of the staff participate in the selection of titles that find a place on the shelves of City Lights. This three-decade-old practice of staff participation is an important part of City Lights's continued relevance and long-term sustainability.

www.citylights.com

PAUL YAMAZAKI, BOOK BUYER

Acquiring books is a craft, and in my forty-three years in the business many things have changed, but the essentials of bookselling have remained the same: reading, curiosity, and conversation. These lie at the heart of what I do. And to the question, who do you trust to recommend books, I would say, I look for the answer in conversation with many people, with independent booksellers around the country, with editors at publishing houses large and small, with publisher sales representatives and with my colleagues at City Lights. Here, the conversation about what books to read and what books will be represented on our shelves begins with the staff. Each member of the City Lights crew participates in the decision over what front list and backlist titles City Lights will offer. And as each person has individual interests, we bring our collective curiosity to bear.

An ongoing dialogue with editors is another key element of City Lights's curatorial practice. We talk to editors to learn about new writers and books, and this, in turn, allows our staff to be early readers and champions of authors and books that have modest announced print runs and marketing and publicity budgets. At City Lights we see this kind of engagement and conversation as essential to what we do, presenting books often not found elsewhere.

Every decade, it seems, has featured a major challenge to the independent bookseller. At City Lights, we manage by being very selective. The craft of bookselling lies not so much in reacting to the marketplace as in developing it by representing, on our shelves, a point of view that sets us apart. As independent booksellers, we build the final plank in the bridge that connects the writer to the reader.

PAUL'S LIST

- [ ] **The Complete Works of Isaac Babel**
- [ ] **The Salt Eaters,** Toni Cade Bambara
- [ ] **The Arcades Project,** Walter Benjamin
- [ ] **Aimé Césaire: The Collected Poetry,** Aimé Césaire
- [ ] **The Long Goodbye,** Raymond Chandler
- [ ] **Below the Line,** Sara Chin
- [ ] **A Secret Location on the Lower East Side,** Steven Clay
- [ ] **City of Quartz: Excavating the Future in Los Angeles,** Mike Davis
- [ ] **Underworld,** Don DeLillo
- [ ] **The Brothers Karamazov,** Fyodor Dostoevsky
- [ ] **Facing West: Metaphysics of Indian-Hating and Empire-Building,** Richard Drinnon
- [ ] **Ark of Bones,** Henry Dumas
- [ ] **A Coney Island of the Mind: Poems,** Lawrence Ferlinghetti
- [ ] **Reconstruction: America's Unfinished Revolution, 1863–1877,** Eric Foner
- [ ] **100 Years of Solitude,** Gabriel Garcia Márquez
- [ ] **Howl,** Allen Ginsberg
- [ ] **The Wind in the Willows,** Kenneth Grahame
- [ ] **Dogeaters,** Jessica Hagedorn

- [ ] **Les Misérables,** Victor Hugo
- [ ] **Black Jacobins: Toussaint L'Ouverture and the San Domingo Revolution,** C. L. R. James
- [ ] **The Known World,** Edward P. Jones
- [ ] **The Black Music,** LeRoi Jones
- [ ] **Blues People,** LeRoi Jones
- [ ] **Ulysses,** James Joyce
- [ ] **Solitudes Crowded with Loneliness,** Bob Kaufman
- [ ] **Thelonius Monk: The Life and Times of an American Original,** Robin D. G. Kelley
- [ ] **Many-Headed Hydra: Sailors, Slaves, Commoners, and the Hidden History of the Revolutionary Atlantic,** Peter Linebaugh and Marcus Rediker
- [ ] **From a Broken Bottle Traces of Perfume Still Emanate,** Nathaniel Mackey
- [ ] **Malcolm X: A Life of Reinvention,** Manning Marable
- [ ] **Battle Cry of Freedom: The Civil War Era,** James McPherson
- [ ] **Moby-Dick,** Herman Melville
- [ ] **Recyclopedia: Trimmings, S*PeRM**K*T, and Muse & Drudge,** Harryette Mullen
- [ ] **The Man Without Qualities,** Robert Musil
- [ ] **No-No Boy,** John Okada
- [ ] **Mumbo Jumbo,** Ishmael Reed
- [ ] **Complete Poems of Kenneth Rexroth**

- [ ] **Midnight's Children,** Salman Rushdie
- [ ] **Orientalism,** Edward Said
- [ ] **God's Bit of Wood,** Ousmane Sembene
- [ ] **River of Shadows: Eadweard Muybridge and the Technical Wild West,** Rebecca Solnit
- [ ] **Four Lives in the Bebop Business,** A. B. Spellman
- [ ] **God's Chinese Son: The Taiping Heavenly Kingdom of Hong Xiuquan,** Jonathan D. Spence
- [ ] **Between Covers: The Rise and Transformation of Book Publishing in America,** John Tebbel
- [ ] **The Making of the English Working Class,** Edward P. Thompson
- [ ] **Flash of the Spirit: African & Afro-American Art & Philosophy,** Robert Farris Thompson
- [ ] **War and Peace,** Leo Tolstoy
- [ ] **Giant Talk: An Anthology of Third World Writings,** Quincy Troupe
- [ ] **My Life in the Bush of Ghosts,** Amos Tutuola
- [ ] **Autobiography of Malcolm X,** Malcolm X
- [ ] **I Hotel,** Karen Tei Yamashita

I decided that the books I selected would be books that helped shaped the way I read, how I perceive the world, and how I helped create the buying system that we have used at City Lights for the past thirty years.

Wind in the Willows by Kenneth Grahame, illustrated by Ernest H. Shepard, is the book that revealed to me the magic of the written word. It is *Wind in the Willows* that sent me down the road of attempting to be a discerning reader, a road that led me to the doors of City Lights, a road that seems to have no end.

Two books acted as the alembic that distilled the barbaric yawp of experience for me. They would provide a deep foundation of ideas and questions that would inform my work as an independent bookseller. C. L. R. James's *Black Jacobins* is one of the finest works of history written in the twentieth century. James's account of the Haitian revolution and the life of Toussaint L'Ouverture is a story of triumph and tragedy that reverberates to this day.

Blues People by LeRoi Jones, now Amiri Baraka, I consider one of the primary works for anyone interested in African American musics. In a language that is as rich and passionate as the music he explores, Jones/Baraka presents the reader with a cohesive framework for understanding the legacy and impact of African American music as well as the broad culture and history of the Americas.

C. L. R. James and Amiri Baraka's skillful analyses, in combination with their passion and commitment to their subjects, illuminated an epistemological path that I still follow today.

Faulkner House Books

NEW ORLEANS, LA

Faulkner House Books was established on September 25, 1990, on William Faulkner's ninety-third birthday. It is a full-service new and used bookstore specializing in fine literature and rare editions, including, of course, books by and about William Faulkner. Faulkner House itself is a national literary landmark. In 1925, the twenty-seven-year-old future Nobel Laureate William Faulkner rented rooms on the ground floor of the building that houses the current store. Other specialties at the store include Tennessee Williams, Walker Percy, eighteenth-century Johnsoniana, modern first editions, and southern Americana with an emphasis on New Orleans and Louisiana-related titles. Faulkner House Books welcomes specials requests and does custom searches for books.

www.faulknerhouse.net

JOSEPH DESALVO, OWNER AND PRESIDENT

On books and bookselling:
Some read to find themselves, others to lose themselves. My reading preferences were set in my youth: an unending fascination with wwii, undoubtedly an outgrowth of a child's yearning to comprehend an event disturbingly larger than himself. The constant attraction of the classics was surely rooted in the four years of Latin and two of Greek studied in a Jesuit high school. There I met Cicero, Virgil, and Homer. Lastly, a felt need to fill the cultural vacuity of an undergraduate degree in business seeded the rest: an enduring, exciting, and never-without-a-book adventure.

A bookseller the last twenty-one of my seventy-nine years, I'm occasionally asked what I was before. "A lawyer," I confess, and add, "Kids often make choices that adults must live with." In fairness, practicing law did enable me in the early seventies to become a serious book collector. Samuel Johnson, James Boswell, and their friends were my long-time literary acquaintances. My favorite haunt, Detering Book Gallery, had two first editions of Boswell's *Life of Samuel Johnson*. One became (and still is) mine.

So why a bookstore? Why not! Before the Internet, an open shop was considered the final stage of the book-collecting disease. In 1988 my wife, Rosemary, and I purchased the building where William Faulkner wrote his first novel. To such uniqueness add antique furnishings, custom cabinets, and bookcases made out of old swamp cypress. Suffuse the space with the shared intelligence and pleasure found in the carefully chosen books, and twenty-one years later Faulkner House Books remains a favorite destination for book lovers.

JOSEPH'S LIST

- [ ] **Mansfield Park,** Jane Austen
- [ ] **Père Goriot,** Honoré de Balzac
- [ ] **Henderson the Rain King,** Saul Bellow
- [ ] **Herzog,** Saul Bellow
- [ ] **The Long Ships,** Frans G. Bengtsson
- [ ] **The Life of Samuel Johnson,** James Boswell
- [ ] **Jane Eyre,** Charlotte Brontë
- [ ] **Wuthering Heights,** Emily Brontë
- [ ] **Death Comes for the Archbishop,** Willa Cather
- [ ] **Don Quixote,** Miguel de Cervantes
- [ ] **Anton Chekhov's Short Stories**
- [ ] **Heart of Darkness,** Joseph Conrad
- [ ] **Nostromo, a Tale of the Seaboard,** Joseph Conrad
- [ ] **The Secret Agent: A Simple Tale,** Joseph Conrad
- [ ] **Out of Africa,** Isak Dinesen
- [ ] **The Brothers Karamazov,** Fyodor Dostoyevsky
- [ ] **Crime and Punishment,** Fyodor Dostoyevsky
- [ ] **Middlemarch,** George Eliot
- [ ] **Invisible Man,** Ralph Ellison
- [ ] **Absalom, Absalom!,** William Faulkner

- [ ] **Light in August,** William Faulkner
- [ ] **The Sound and the Fury,** William Faulkner
- [ ] **The Great Gatsby,** F. Scott Fitzgerald
- [ ] **Madame Bovary,** Gustave Flaubert
- [ ] **The Good Soldier,** Ford Madox Ford
- [ ] **Dead Souls,** Nikolai Gogol
- [ ] **Life and Fate,** Vasily Grossman
- [ ] **The Complete Short Stories of Ernest Hemingway**
- [ ] **The Old Man and the Sea,** Ernest Hemingway
- [ ] **The Odyssey and The Iliad,** Homer
- [ ] **Zorba the Greek,** Nikos Kazantzakis
- [ ] **The Leopard,** Giuseppe Tomasi di Lampedusa
- [ ] **The Balkan Trilogy,** Olivia Manning
- [ ] **Moby-Dick,** Herman Melville
- [ ] **History,** Elsa Morante
- [ ] **Lolita,** Vladimir Nabokov
- [ ] **The Moviegoer,** Walker Percy
- [ ] **The Radetzky March,** Joseph Roth
- [ ] **Crossing to Safety,** Wallace Stegner
- [ ] **The Red and the Black,** Stendhal
- [ ] **Sophie's Choice,** William Styron
- [ ] **Anna Karenina,** Leo Tolstoy
- [ ] **The Death of Ivan Ilyich,** Leo Tolstoy

- [ ] **War and Peace,** Leo Tolstoy
- [ ] **A Confederacy of Dunces,** John Kennedy Toole
- [ ] **The Adventures of Huckleberry Finn,** Mark Twain
- [ ] **Rabbit Angstrom: The Four Novels,** John Updike
- [ ] **The Aeneid,** Virgil
- [ ] **All the King's Men,** Robert Penn Warren
- [ ] **The Optimist's Daughter,** Eudora Welty

Don Quixote, Miguel de Cervantes
The wellspring of the modern novel, frequently imitated but never equaled. Cervantes's mad hero, more admirable than his adversaries, refuses to let his eyes and ears set limits on his world. This book was a favorite of Samuel Johnson and also of William Faulkner, who was once asked, wasn't it too long? His response was that he hadn't noticed.

Life of Samuel Johnson, James Boswell
Boswell, a worldly, intelligent, and curious lawyer, writes about a prodigious and eccentric genius. Dr. Johnson, son of a bookseller, lived most of his seventy-five years in London. With his writing and his talking, he became the literary center of a neoclassical period of enlightenment before the revolutions began. Oliver Goldsmith, Edward Gibbon, Edmund Burke, David Garrick, James Boswell, and countless others populate the pages of *Life*. Beware: the eighteenth century is easier entered than left.

War and Peace, Leo Tolstoy
Years ago in an AT&T advertisement, some device, now obsolete, was pictured on the left of the copy with the caption, "This is Easy." On the right was a mock edition

of *War and Peace*, labeled, "This is Hard." The copy-writer, I dare say, never read the book. It's not hard. It is long but richly full of memorable characters caught up in a horrific war against Napoleon. I have read *War and Peace* several times. Once, after turning the last page, I immediately returned to the beginning and read it again.

Nostromo, a Tale of the Seaboard, Joseph Conrad

In his Nobel Prize speech, Saul Bellow confessed that as a young man he had spent more time reading Conrad's books than his school texts, and that he never had any regrets. My Conrad favorite is *Nostromo*. Its characters live their lives against the backdrop of an affecting revolution. Robert Penn Warren, also a fan, felt *Nostromo* rightfully earned a place on the shelf next to *War and Peace*.

Fireside Books

PALMER, AK

Fireside Books was created by book-loving husband-and-wife team David Cheezem and Melissa Behnke in 2001 to be "a place where good writing was honored and celebrated." Fireside Books carries new and used children's books, young adults books, romance, religion, mystery, reference, nonfiction, Alaskana, how-to, and travel books. They also carry art, postcards, and music from local artists. Ebeart, a stuffed bear (a.k.a. E-bear) can be spotted at Fireside Books in a corner chair with a book in his paws. He is maybe the world's first bookish, blogging bear.

www.goodbooksbadcoffee.com

On being a bookseller:

Working at a bookstore can sometimes feel like performing a parlor trick.

CUSTOMER: "I can't remember the author's name, or title, but I think it's Japanese. I remember the cover really well, though: it's blue, with flower petals or snowflakes or something on it. Or maybe numbers."

BOOKSELLER: "Is it . . . *The Housekeeper and the Professor,* by Yoko Ogawa?"

I love to think of it as a kind of bookish superhero power, but it's really a matter of knowing the stock, being familiar with many genres, and listening to what customers and booksellers say.

But in a few very special cases, handselling is nothing like a parlor trick. Sometimes when I'm at home reading a book (*A Reliable Wife,* by Robert Goolrick), before I've turned the last page I know precisely the favorite customer who is going to love it. Sometimes as I'm swept up in a story (*The Raven's Gift,* by Don Rearden), half my joy comes from thinking about the people who will be moved and changed by it.

"Here," I say the next day, and I take the book from the shelf and place it gently in the customer's hands. "Read this."

It is a small but heartfelt gift, one reader to another.

EOWYN'S LIST

- [ ] **Things Fall Apart,** Chinua Achebe
- [ ] **Ship Breaker,** Paolo Bacigalupi
- [ ] **Peter Pan,** J. M. Barrie
- [ ] **Goodnight Moon,** Margaret Wise Brown, illustrated by Clement Hurd
- [ ] **The Good Earth,** Pearl S. Buck
- [ ] **My Life in France,** Julia Child with Alex Prud'homme
- [ ] **The Green Age of Asher Witherow,** M. Allen Cunningham
- [ ] **And Her Soul Out of Nothing,** Olena Kalytiak Davis
- [ ] **The Brief Wondrous Life of Oscar Wao,** Junot Díaz
- [ ] **What Is the What,** Dave Eggers
- [ ] **Love Medicine,** Louise Erdrich
- [ ] **The Spirit Catches You and You Fall Down,** Anne Fadiman
- [ ] **As I Lay Dying,** William Faulkner
- [ ] **Then We Came to the End,** Joshua Ferris
- [ ] **Crooked Letter, Crooked Letter,** Tom Franklin
- [ ] **Cold Mountain,** Charles Frazier
- [ ] **The Art of Fielding,** Chad Harbach
- [ ] **Tinkers,** Paul Harding

- [ ] **Winter's Tale,** Mark Helprin
- [ ] **The Complete Short Stories of Ernest Hemingway**
- [ ] **The Age of Wonder: How the Romantic Generation Discovered the Beauty and Terror of Science,** Richard Holmes
- [ ] **Ordinary Wolves,** Seth Kantner
- [ ] **Diary of a Wimpy Kid,** Jeff Kinney
- [ ] **Adventures of Cow,** Lori Korchek, photographs by Marshall Taylor
- [ ] **All the Powerful Invisible Things: A Sportswoman's Notebook,** Gretchen Legler
- [ ] **A Wrinkle in Time,** Madeleine L'Engle
- [ ] **The Giver,** Lois Lowry
- [ ] **Life of Pi,** Yann Martel
- [ ] **Let the Great World Spin,** Colum McCann
- [ ] **All the Pretty Horses,** Cormac McCarthy
- [ ] **If Nobody Speaks of Remarkable Things,** Jon McGregor
- [ ] **Lonesome Dove,** Larry McMurtry
- [ ] **The River of Doubt: Theodore Roosevelt's Darkest Journey,** Candice Millard
- [ ] **A Fine Balance,** Rohinton Mistry
- [ ] **Beloved,** Toni Morrison
- [ ] **Two in the Far North,** Margaret E. Murie
- [ ] **Suite Française,** Irene Nemirovsky

- [ ] **The Things They Carried,** Tim O'Brien
- [ ] **True Grit,** Charles Portis
- [ ] **The Shipping News,** Annie Proulx
- [ ] **Housekeeping,** Marilynne Robinson
- [ ] **The Spanish Bow,** Andromeda Romano-Lax
- [ ] **Frankenstein,** Mary Shelley
- [ ] **Balzac and the Little Chinese Seamstress,** Dai Sijie
- [ ] **Angle of Repose,** Wallace Stegner
- [ ] **The Art of Racing in the Rain,** Garth Stein
- [ ] **The Ice-Shirt (Seven Dreams),** William T. Vollmann
- [ ] **Two Old Women: An Alaska Legend of Betrayal, Courage and Survival,** Velma Wallis
- [ ] **We Are in a Book!,** Mo Willems
- [ ] **Stoner,** John Williams

The one book I was certain had to be on my list was Louise Erdrich's *Love Medicine,* and it was from purely selfish motives—it's the novel that made me want to be a better writer. I first read it in college, and to this day it leaves me in awe. I recommend it to customers I think will appreciate its lyrical, heartbreaking power.

Many books on my recommended list share this element—beautifully poetic novels like *The Green Age of Asher Witherow, Tinkers, Housekeeping.* But as both a reader and bookseller, I like to balance that with humor and surprise. *The Brief Wondrous Life of Oscar Wao* and *Then We Came to the End* made me laugh out loud, which I rarely do when reading, but ultimately they stunned me. I can ask no more of a novel.

The book that might be closest to my heart, though, is *Goodnight Moon.* A friend gave me a board-book edition of this classic children's story when our first daughter was born. My husband and I read it to her again and again, until the corners were worn and the words were like old friends. Eight years later, when our second daughter was born, we still had that original copy. Now we read those same pages to her, watching the little green room slowly darken into night.

When customers come to Fireside Books in search of a baby present, I can think of no better gift than the love of books; I hand them *Goodnight Moon.*

Harvard Book Store

CAMBRIDGE, MA

Harvard Book Store is an independently run bookstore serving the greater Cambridge area. The bookstore is located in Harvard Square and has been family owned since 1932. Harvard Book Store is known for their extraordinary selection of new, used, and bargain books and for a history of innovation. In 2009, they introduced same-day environmentally friendly bike delivery and a book-making robot called Paige M. Guttenborg capable of printing and binding any of millions of titles in minutes.

www.harvard.com

MEGAN SULLIVAN, HEAD BUYER

Who is your most trusted source for book recommendations?
I trust my fellow booksellers both at HBS and at other independent stores. I've had numerous recommendations from them that have worked out wonderfully.

What's your favorite bookstore (other than the one you work at)?
It doesn't exist anymore, but Davis and Kidd in Nashville was one of the first stores I went to that completely overwhelmed me with the sheer size of their stock. As a kid, I found it a magical place.

What is one thing about bookselling most people do not know?
Do you know how often Jack Kerouac books are shoplifted?

What book is on your nightstand right now?
Currently I'm working on *Zona,* by Geoff Dyer. I love him.

MEGAN'S LIST

- [ ] **The Hitchhiker's Guide to the Galaxy,** Douglas Adams
- [ ] **Little Women,** Louisa May Alcott
- [ ] **The Divine Comedy,** Dante Alighieri
- [ ] **The Handmaid's Tale,** Margaret Atwood
- [ ] **Pride and Prejudice,** Jane Austen
- [ ] **Ficciones,** Jorge Luis Borges
- [ ] **Jane Eyre,** Charlotte Brontë
- [ ] **The Master and Margarita,** Mikhail Bulgakov
- [ ] **If on a Winter's Night a Traveler,** Italo Calvino
- [ ] **Alice's Adventures in Wonderland/Through the Looking Glass,** Lewis Carroll
- [ ] **The Amazing Adventures of Kavalier and Clay,** Michael Chabon
- [ ] **White Noise,** Don DeLillo
- [ ] **Great Expectations,** Charles Dickens
- [ ] **Slouching Towards Bethlehem,** Joan Didion
- [ ] **Crime and Punishment,** Fyodor Dostoevsky
- [ ] **Middlemarch,** George Eliot
- [ ] **Invisible Man,** Ralph Ellison
- [ ] **The Sound and the Fury,** William Faulkner
- [ ] **The Great Gatsby,** F. Scott Fitzgerald

- [ ] **One Hundred Years of Solitude,** Gabriel García Márquez
- [ ] **Sea of Poppies,** Amitav Ghosh
- [ ] **Catch 22,** Joseph Heller
- [ ] **A Moveable Feast,** Ernest Hemingway
- [ ] **The Histories,** Herodotus
- [ ] **A Prayer for Owen Meany,** John Irving
- [ ] **Dubliners,** James Joyce
- [ ] **The Phantom Tollbooth,** Norton Juster
- [ ] **Mountains Beyond Mountains,** Tracy Kidder
- [ ] **To Kill a Mockingbird,** Harper Lee
- [ ] **The Earthsea Cycle** (series), Ursula K. Le Guin
- [ ] **A Wrinkle in Time,** Madeleine L'Engle
- [ ] **The Heart Is a Lonely Hunter,** Carson McCullers
- [ ] **Beloved,** Toni Morrison
- [ ] **Wild Sheep Chase,** Haruki Murakami
- [ ] **The Wind-Up Bird Chronicle,** Haruki Murakami
- [ ] **Their Eyes Were Watching God,** Zora Neale Hurston
- [ ] **Lolita,** Vladimir Nabokov
- [ ] **The Bell Jar,** Sylvia Plath
- [ ] **His Dark Materials** (series), Philip Pullman
- [ ] **Housekeeping,** Marilynne Robinson
- [ ] **Harry Potter** (series), J. K. Rowling

- ☐ **Midnight's Children,** Salman Rushdie
- ☐ **Cannery Row,** John Steinbeck
- ☐ **The Lord of the Rings** (series), J. R. R. Tolkien
- ☐ **Anna Karenina,** Leo Tolstoy
- ☐ **Breakfast of Champions,** Kurt Vonnegut
- ☐ **Cat's Cradle,** Kurt Vonnegut
- ☐ **Mrs. Dalloway,** Virginia Woolf
- ☐ **To the Lighthouse,** Virginia Woolf
- ☐ **Dealing with Dragons,** Patricia Wrede

Jane Eyre, Charlotte Brontë
This is a favorite not only of mine but many of the book-sellers here at Harvard Book Store. The story of a strong young woman trying to make her way in the world is a hard plotline to resist!

Middlemarch, George Eliot
I was a latecomer to *Middlemarch,* having read it for the first time only five years ago. It's still one of the five best books I've ever read.

Slouching Towards Bethlehem, Joan Didion
Didion's book exemplifies what the essay can do for nonfiction. Not only a portrait of the sixties, *Slouching* remains some of the best prose on the shelves today.

Inkwood Books

TAMPA, FL

Opened in 1991, Inkwood Books is Tampa's only full-service independent bookstore. Located in a twenties bungalow, the "small but mighty" Inkwood offers a handpicked selection from the popular to the obscure. Their strengths include fiction, children's books, politics and current events, biography, poetry, cookbooks, and Floridiana. The bookstore hosts book signings and discussions by local and national authors, supplies course readings for students, and supports countless local charities. Inkwood Books founded the Tampa Independent Business Alliance, pioneered the now national Independents Week campaign, and believes in shopping locally to "keep Tampa authentic."

www.inkwoodbooks.com

CARLA JIMENEZ, CO-OWNER

What book is on your nightstand right now?
I am juggling Walter Mosley's *All I Did Was Shoot My Man* and S. C. Gwynne's *Empire of the Summer Moon: Quanah Parker and the Rise and Fall of the Commanches, the Most Powerful Tribe in American History*. Next in the stack is an advance copy of John Irving's *In One Person*.

What is one thing about bookselling most people don't know?
The joy of exposure to so many great books is tempered by sadness over the impossibility of finding enough time to read.

Which book on your list do you think is particularly underrated?
Today I'd pick Philipp Meyers's *American Rust* in fiction, for its heart-wrenching truth of blue-collar hopelessness. And for nonfiction, I wish everyone would shout about the persuasive and compellingly lovely small book by David Ulin, *The Lost Art of Reading: Why Books Matter in a Distracted Time*.

Who is your most trusted source for book recommendations?
I am grateful to still have a local book editor, Colette Bancroft of the *Tampa Bay Times* (formerly *St. Petersburg*

Times), whose favorites almost always match my own. And I trust those reading friends—including customers who have thereby become friends—who have equal passion for books I have embraced. Finally, the *New York Times* Notables list has so often included non–best sellers that I have loved, so I follow their lead to anything I've missed.

CARLA'S LIST

- [ ] **I Thought My Father Was God: And Other True Tales from NPR's National Story Project,** edited by Paul Auster

- [ ] **The Secret Names of Women,** Lynne Barrett

- [ ] **The Feast of Love,** Charles Baxter

- [ ] **Grub,** Elise Blackwell

- [ ] **A Blind Man Can See How Much I Love You,** Amy Bloom

- [ ] **Father and Son,** Larry Brown

- [ ] **Comfortable with Uncertainty: 108 Teachings on Cultivating Fearlessness and Compassion,** Pema Chödrön

- [ ] **The Year of Magical Thinking,** Joan Didion

- [ ] **Sister of My Heart,** Chitra Benerjee Divakaruni

- [ ] **The March,** E. L. Doctorow

- [ ] **Ella Minnow Pea,** Mark Dunn

- [ ] **The Gathering,** Anne Enright

- [ ] **Before Women Had Wings,** Connie May Fowler

- [ ] **Dreaming in Cuban,** Cristina Garcia

- [ ] **Under Cover of Daylight,** James W. Hall

- [ ] **In Praise of Slowness: Challenging the Cult of Speed,** Carl Honore

- [ ] **Round Rock,** Michelle Huneven
- [ ] **Listening Is an Act of Love: A Celebration of American Life from the StoryCorps Project,** Dave Isay
- [ ] **Exuberance: The Passion for Life,** Kay Redfield Jamison
- [ ] **The Liars' Club,** Mary Karr
- [ ] **The Poisonwood Bible,** Barbara Kingsolver
- [ ] **The Namesake,** Jhumpa Lahiri
- [ ] **Bird by Bird: Some Instructions on Writing and Life,** Annie Lamott
- [ ] **The Surrendered,** Chang-Rae Lee
- [ ] **Mystic River,** Dennis Lehane
- [ ] **Last Child in the Woods: Saving Our Children from Nature-Deficit Disorder,** Richard Luov
- [ ] **Men Giving Money, Women Yelling,** Alice Mattison
- [ ] **Deep Economy: The Wealth of Communities and the Durable Future,** Bill McKibben
- [ ] **Assorted Fire Events,** David Means
- [ ] **In Cuba I Was a German Shepherd,** Ana Menéndez
- [ ] **American Rust,** Philipp Meyer
- [ ] **Big-Box Swindle: The True Cost of Mega-Retailers and the Fight for America's Independent Businesses,** Stacy Mitchell
- [ ] **The Tender Bar,** J. R. Moehringer
- [ ] **Suite Française,** Irene Nemirovsky

- [ ] **The Book of Awakening: Having the Life You Want by Being Present to the Life You Have,** Mark Nepo
- [ ] **The Bird Artist,** Howard Norman
- [ ] **Prayers for Healing: 365 Blessings, Poems & Meditations from Around the World,** Maggie Oman et al.
- [ ] **The Well and the Mine,** Gin Phillips
- [ ] **Lush Life,** Richard Price
- [ ] **Nobody's Fool,** Richard Russo
- [ ] **Fast Food Nation: The Dark Side of the All-American Meal,** Eric Schlosser
- [ ] **Snow Flower and the Secret Fan,** Lisa See
- [ ] **Larry's Party,** Carol Shields
- [ ] **The Immortal Life of Henrietta Lacks,** Rebecca Skloot
- [ ] **White Teeth,** Zadie Smith
- [ ] **The Little Friend,** Donna Tartt
- [ ] **Ultimate Punishment: A Lawyer's Reflections on Dealing with the Death Penalty,** Scott Turow
- [ ] **The Lost Art of Reading: Why Books Matter in a Distracted Time,** David L. Ulin
- [ ] **The Warmth of Other Suns: The Epic Story of America's Great Migration,** Isabel Wilkerson
- [ ] **Breath,** Tim Winton

Grub, Elise Blackwell
Really smart—and a little snarky—*Grub* has true-to-life authors with friendships forged in creative writing workshops, then sorely tested as competition sets in. Spot-on descriptions of author tours, arguments about commercialism versus true art, and a love triangle add to the entertainment—especially for book business insiders.

Comfortable with Uncertainty: 108 Teachings on Cultivating Fearlessness and Compassion, Pema Chödrön
This is my go-to gift for anyone facing illness or other challenges, and is always welcome, with the Buddhist nun's lessons on mindfulness and compassion emphasizing acceptance and letting go of fear.

Ella Minnow Pea, Mark Dunn
This is a clever cautionary tale with lessons about power and rebellion in epistolary form. As alphabet letters fall off the wall commemorating the man known for devising the "quick red fox" sentence, civic leaders outlaw use of the missing letters. The diminished alphabet makes the correspondence especially interesting and fun, with a brave teacher and earnest investigative reporter writing in code and fighting the good fight.

Before Women Had Wings, Connie May Fowler

This semiautobiographical story of a curious young girl neglected by her troubled mother, who learns about life—and books—from a generous and gentle woman, is beautifully crafted, with heartbreak and tenderness and a Tampa setting.

Ultimate Punishment: A Lawyer's Reflections on Dealing with the Death Penalty, Scott Turow

I love his legal thrillers, but especially cherish this important and brilliantly written nonfiction gem. With even-handed presentation of both sides, Turow takes us on his journey from capital punishment supporter to activist against the penalty after serving on the Illinois commission whose report led to commutation of dozens of sentences. With his personal experience as both prosecutor and defense attorney, Turow may be the ultimate persuader on the ultimate punishment.

Iowa Book

IOWA CITY, IA

Independent booksellers serving Iowa City and the University of Iowa since 1920, Iowa Book has a selection of popular fiction titles, including signed editions and a textbook rental program.

www.iowabook.com

What's the oddest book request or question you've received from a customer?

Hoary stories abound. When Paul Ingram of Prairie Lights worked here, he maintained that a student requested a copy of *The Elephants of Style* by Trunk and White, though my colleagues believe him to be fibbing. We were asked for, variously, *A Fellow* by Shakespeare and *The Eyelid* of Homer. Maintaining a deadpan expression is mandatory in this gig.

What book on your list do you feel is underrated?

I don't think any of the titles (or authors) are underrated, more unappreciated. One doesn't have to trumpet the Don Delillos or Zadie Smiths, but short story writers—and my list is lousy with them—need a bit more of a push. J. F. Powers wrote almost exclusively about priests, and if you're not a (lapsed) Papist like me, who cares? But his stories are gorgeously written, very funny, and provide wonderful insights into the human character. Is there a more perfect short story than "In the Garden Where Al Jolson Is Buried," by Amy Hempel? "In the White Night," by Ann Beattie? In the eighties, Wright Morris seemed to be ubiquitous in the annual *Best American Short Stories*. There's a good reason why. Nobody seems to read Frank O'Connor anymore, thus missing out on how a master can make sentences dance. And writers like Peter Cameron and David Leavitt are writing only novels these days; I miss the refreshing dispatches of their early short stories. Finally, if you even remotely have a sense of humor, you should have read *The Colony of Unrequited Dreams* by now.

MATTHEW'S LIST

☐ **The Untouchable,** John Banville

☐ **The Regeneration Trilogy,** Pat Barker

☐ **The Whereabouts of Eneas McNulty,** Sebastian Barry

☐ **The New Yorker Stories,** Ann Beattie

☐ **Untold Stories,** Alan Bennett

☐ **Any Human Heart,** William Boyd

☐ **Earthly Powers,** Anthony Burgess

☐ **The Half You Don't Know: Selected Stories,**
   Peter Cameron

☐ **The Yiddish Policemen's Union,** Michael Chabon

☐ **The Stories of John Cheever**

☐ **Underworld,** Don DeLillo

☐ **A Star Called Henry,** Roddy Doyle

☐ **The Virgin Suicides,** Jeffrey Eugenides

☐ **The Collected Stories of Mavis Gallant**

☐ **The Story of a Marriage,** Andrew Sean Greer

☐ **The Practical Heart: Four Novellas,** Allan Gurganus

☐ **The Short History of a Prince,** Jane Hamilton

☐ **The Collected Stories of Amy Hempel**

☐ **The Complete Ripley Novels,** Patricia Highsmith

☐ **The Stranger's Child,** Alan Hollinghurst

- [ ] **The Swimming-Pool Library,** Alan Hollinghurst
- [ ] **The Remains of the Day,** Kazuo Ishiguro
- [ ] **The Colony of Unrequited Dreams,** Wayne Johnston
- [ ] **The Known World,** Edward P. Jones
- [ ] **The Quest for Karla,** John Le Carré
- [ ] **Collected Stories,** David Leavitt
- [ ] **Collected Stories,** Frank O'Connor
- [ ] **At Swim, Two Boys,** Jamie O'Neill
- [ ] **No Great Mischief,** Alistair MacLeod
- [ ] **Charming Billy,** Alice McDermott
- [ ] **Atonement,** Ian McEwan
- [ ] **Black Swan Green,** David Mitchell
- [ ] **The Collected Stories,** Lorrie Moore
- [ ] **Collected Stories,** Wright Morris
- [ ] **Selected Stories,** Alice Munro
- [ ] **The Ghosts of Belfast,** Stuart Neville
- [ ] **The Francoeur Novels: The Family, The Woods, The Country,** David Plante
- [ ] **The Collected Stories of J. F. Powers**
- [ ] **A Cab at the Door & Midnight Oil,** V. S. Pritchett
- [ ] **Close Range: Wyoming Stories,** Annie Proulx
- [ ] **White Teeth,** Zadie Smith
- [ ] **Olive Kitteridge,** Elizabeth Strout

- [ ] **Last Orders,** Graham Swift
- [ ] **The Early Stories: 1953–1975,** John Updike
- [ ] **William Trevor: The Collected Stories**
- [ ] **United States,** Gore Vidal
- [ ] **The Complete Short Stories,** Evelyn Waugh
- [ ] **The Farewell Symphony,** Edmund White
- [ ] **The Best of Wodehouse,** P. G. Wodehouse

My reading habits as an adolescent were dreck-complacent: lots of comic books and Doc Savage paperbacks. It wasn't until age eighteen and having my first lit class in college that I was exposed to John Cheever's "The Country Husband" in an anthology. That was my Saul-on-the-road-to-Damascus moment: that fiction could be clever, entertaining, and sharply written. Everything I've read in the ensuing thirty-seven years can be traced to that story.

There are three living masters of the short story: William Trevor, Alice Munro, and Mavis Gallant, and their respective collecteds are my desert island choices; lots of bang for the buck and always something new to discover upon rereading. Chabon's *Yiddish Policeman's Union* is a howler; I still remember reading it on a cold March day and hooting aloud at the sentences and wondering at his effortless jazzy improvisation—will he ever be able to top it? Finally, there isn't a lot of notable gay fiction published these days; like its hetero brethren, a lot of it can be dismissed. So thank you to Alan Hollinghurst, whose *Swimming-Pool Library* and *The Stranger's Child* are both wonderfully evocative of their times and beautifully crafted, and Jamie O'Neill's vastly underappreciated *At Swim, Two Boys,* a novel set during the Easter Uprising of 1916 that, shorn of sentimentality, is a moving love story.

The King's English Bookshop

SALT LAKE CITY, UT

Located in a residential neighborhood of Salt Lake City, the King's English Bookshop has been offering a diverse range of books since 1977, including mysteries, fiction, poetry, literary nonfiction, nature, books about the West, and of course, all kinds of books for children. With eight book-packed rooms, the King's English contains delightful surprises around every corner, including a secret staircase to the mystery room! Co-owner and co-founder Betsy Burton is active in Local First Utah and her book, *The King's English: Adventures of an Independent Bookseller,* is a love story to the trials and tribulations of running an indie bookstore. The store hosts hundreds of author events each year, supports dozens of local charities through in-kind donations, and sponsors countless hours of children's events throughout each year. In short, it does what all indies do: makes its community better!

www.kingsenglish.com

BETSY BURTON, OWNER

What book is on your nightstand right now?
I have never, not once, had just one book on my night-stand. In fact, the pile that perpetually resides there, threatening to topple (it's happened more than once), not to mention the mounds that I nestle among on my bed, may, along with my habit of turning on the light to read at two a.m., be the reason my husband fled screaming to the guest bedroom years ago.

Right now the pile by my lamp consists of six books (*All That I Am,* by Anna Funder is far and away my favorite of this batch) for which I'm writing radio reviews. There's also Terry Tempest Williams's *When Women Were Birds,* which I'm reading for the second time; it's not just brilliant but, as always, different from anything she's done before. There are a few I'm dying to read strewn across the bed: the new Mark Haddon (I'm hoping against hope I'll like it as much as his first two); new books by Alain de Botton and William Boyd; Ann Tyler's new novel; and Donna Leon's latest (her mysteries are liquid heroin to my mind); along with assorted mysteries old and new, in case I need another fix. Finally, there are two books on books by Michael Dirda that I've meant to read for months, and will soon!

Who needs Ambien or hot-water bottles when there are books by—or in—the bed? Not me—or any book-seller I know.

LIST FROM THE BOOKSELLERS AT THE KING'S ENGLISH BOOKSHOP

- [ ] **Graceland,** Christopher Abani
- [ ] **Before Night Falls,** Reinaldo Arenas
- [ ] **The Guernsey Literary and Potato Peel Pie Society,** Annie Barrows and Mary Ann Schaefer
- [ ] **Bottom of the 33rd: Hope, Redemption, and Baseball's Longest Game,** Dan Barry
- [ ] **City of Thieves,** David Benioff
- [ ] **Amulet,** Roberto Bolaño
- [ ] **The Bricklayer,** Noah Boyd
- [ ] **The Western Lands,** William Burroughs
- [ ] **The Chihuahua Chase,** A. E. Cannon, illustrated by Julie Olsin
- [ ] **Where I'm Calling From,** Raymond Carver
- [ ] **My Ántonia,** Willa Cather
- [ ] **Girls Don't Fly,** Kristen Chandler
- [ ] **Wolves, Boys, and Other Things That Might Kill Me,** Kristen Chandler
- [ ] **Little Bee,** Chris Cleave
- [ ] **Goodnight, Me,** Andrew Daddo, illustrated by Emma Quay
- [ ] **The Madonnas of Leningrad,** Debra Dean

- [ ] **The Marriage Plot,** Jeffrey Eugenides
- [ ] **Charms for the Easy Life,** Kaye Gibbons
- [ ] **Three Junes,** Julia Glass
- [ ] **1861: The Civil War Awakening,** Adam Goodheart
- [ ] **Scapegoat: The Story of a Goat Named Oat and a Chewed-Up Coat,** Dean Hale
- [ ] **The Beekeeper's Apprentice: Or On the Segregation of the Queen,** Laurie R. King
- [ ] **Icefall,** Matthew Kirby
- [ ] **The Juniper Berry,** M. P. Kozlowsky, illustrated by Erwin Madrid
- [ ] **Turn of Mind,** Alice LaPlante
- [ ] **The Surrendered,** Chang-Rae Lee
- [ ] **Suicide,** Edouard Levé
- [ ] **Border Songs,** Jim Lynch
- [ ] **The Highest Tide,** Jim Lynch
- [ ] **The Wake of Forgiveness,** Bruce Machart
- [ ] **Uncivil Seasons,** Michael Malone
- [ ] **Ransom,** David Malouf
- [ ] **A Place of Greater Safety,** Hilary Mantel
- [ ] **Wolf Hall,** Hilary Mantel
- [ ] **Let the Great World Spin,** Colum McCann
- [ ] **The Three Questions,** Jon J. Muth
- [ ] **The Tiger's Wife,** Téa Obreht

- [ ] **Last Night at the Lobster,** Stewart O'Nan
- [ ] **Foreign Bodies,** Cynthia Ozick
- [ ] **The Unlikely Romance of Kate Bjorkman,** Louise Plummer
- [ ] **Miss Peregrine's Home for Peculiar Children,** Ransom Riggs
- [ ] **Firmin,** Sam Savage
- [ ] **Wonderstruck,** Brian Selznick
- [ ] **Olive Kitteridge,** Elizabeth Strout
- [ ] **This Is Where I Leave You,** Jonathon Tropper
- [ ] **The Tiger: A True Story of Vengeance and Survival,** John Vaillant
- [ ] **The Running Dream,** Wendelin Van Draanen
- [ ] **Cutting for Stone,** Abraham Verghese
- [ ] **Motel Life,** Willy Vlautin
- [ ] **How to Save a Life,** Sara Zarr

MORE ABOUT THE KING'S ENGLISH BOOKSHOP'S LIST BY BETSY BURTON

There is something for everyone on the shelves of any independent bookstore. Our art as booksellers lies in matching those books to readers who will like them. Would I recommend *Turn of Mind* by Alice LaPlante to someone who prefers plot-driven fiction? No, but I'd give it to those who like books driven by character. Retired from medicine and living at home with a full-time care-giver, brilliant surgeon Jennifer White slip-slides in and out of dementia, her mind a kaleidoscope of memories merging continually with present-day reality. She is also chief suspect in the murder of her best friend. LaPlante resorts to neither cliché nor soft sentiment, yet manages to profoundly affect—and electrify—the reader.

For those who like their novels largely told yet involved in worlds that are closely examined, *Wolf Hall,* like *Turn of Mind,* is limited to a single viewpoint—but the mind of Thomas Cromwell, entirely rational and unfailingly brilliant, has a firm grip on reality. Complex, secretive, a brilliant tactician, and the right hand of Henry VIII, Cromwell is both witness to and actor in Tudor history in a Booker Prize–winning book.

A novel for those who cherish the small and finely wrought is *Last Night at the Lobster* by Stewart O'Nan, a lovely, quiet gem of a novel that takes place on the final night that a chain restaurant is open for business and manages to juxtapose the touching decency of the men and women who work there with the callousness of its corporate closing. For those who enjoy the classics and the most wonderful of writing, *Ransom,* by David Malouf, is the retelling of the story of the death of Hector and of the brutalizing of his body by Achilles, of King Priam and his journey out of Troy and into the enemy camp to rescue his son's battered body. The sentences literally make the hair on the back of your neck stand up, while the revelations make you reconsider things you thought you knew. Finally, for those who like to laugh, Jonathan Tropper's *This Is Where I Leave You* is ideal.

Magers and Quinn

MINNEAPOLIS, MN

Magers and Quinn is an independently owned new and used bookseller located in the heart of the popular Uptown neighborhood in Minneapolis, near the lakes for which the city is famous. Since opening its doors in 1994, the eight-thousand-square-foot store has been a haven for booklovers across the Midwest. Magers and Quinn stocks a wide array of new, discount, used, and rare titles, with everything from current bestsellers to seventeenth-century relics, and hosts nearly a hundred in-store author events each year.

www.magersandquinn.com

JAY D. PETERSON, STORE MANAGER

What book is on your nightstand right now?
Book? As if there would only be one! *The Collected Poems of T. S. Eliot 1901–1962* and *Collected Poems of George Seferis* are mainstays. Joining them this month are *Uncanny Valley: Adventures in the Narrative* by the amazing Lawrence Weschler, and *Norwegian Wood: The Thoughtful Architecture of Wenche Selmer,* which has me dreaming of retiring to a cozy, fjord-side cabin somewhere outside of Oslo.

What makes a bookstore successful in today's world?
Good neighbors. I don't know where we'd be if it weren't for some of the other merchants on our end of the block. There's a spice shop, a paper shop, a kitchen supply store, and one of the city's finest restaurants, Lucia's, which basically serves as the staff canteen. Each of them attracts a demographic that believes in the power of the printed word and is super supportive of small businesses.

What book made you fall in love with reading?
I read loads of sports fiction and Hardy Boys mysteries as a child, but it was *Coming Home Crazy: An Alphabet of China Essays* by Bill Holm (a Christmas gift received in my late teens) that ultimately did me in. Holm, who passed away in 2009, was truly a remarkable human

being. No other writer has made a greater impact on my reading life.

What is one thing about bookselling most people don't know?

Well, I guess our store is different than most, but I use a forklift and a pallet jack far more than I ever imagined I would. He's never said as much, but I suspect this makes my father deeply proud.

What's the oddest book request or question you've received from a customer?

It's nice to be known as a community resource of information, but phone calls regarding our opinions on certain films, the pronunciation of certain words, or the duration of a parade taking place in an entirely different part of the city seem like a bit of a stretch. That said, if you don't have a smart phone or the internet and you *need* to know who the twenty-third president was in order to settle a dispute, give us a call.

- [ ] **Eucalyptus,** Murray Bail
- [ ] **Anything by John Banville**
- [ ] **Gourmet Rhapsody,** Muriel Barbery
- [ ] **The Best Recipes in the World,** Mark Bittman
- [ ] **Kafka Was the Rage: A Greenwich Village Memoir,** Anatole Broyard
- [ ] **Heat: An Amateur's Adventures as Kitchen Slave, Line Cook, Pasta-Maker, and Apprentice to a Dante-Quoting Butcher in Tuscany,** Bill Buford
- [ ] **Difficult Loves,** Italo Calvino
- [ ] **If on a Winter's Night a Traveler,** Italo Calvino
- [ ] **The Amazing Adventures of Kavalier and Clay,** Michael Chabon
- [ ] **Slouching Towards Bethlehem,** Joan Didion
- [ ] **The Dud Avocado,** Elaine Dundy
- [ ] **A Visit from the Goon Squad,** Jennifer Egan
- [ ] **What is the What,** Dave Eggers
- [ ] **Four Quartets,** T. S. Eliot
- [ ] **River Cottage Every Day,** Hugh Fearnley-Whittingstall
- [ ] **The Basil and Josephine Stories,** F. Scott Fitzgerald
- [ ] **This Side of Paradise,** F. Scott Fitzgerald

95

☐ **Gerhard Richter: Overpainted Photographs,** Gerhard Richter et al.

☐ **Parisians: An Adventure History of Paris,** Graham Robb

☐ **Home,** Marilynne Robinson

☐ **Housekeeping,** Marilynne Robinson

☐ **Gilead,** Marilynne Robinson

☐ **George Seferis: Collected Poems**

☐ **The Invention of Hugo Cabret,** Brian Selznick

☐ **Canoeing with the Cree,** Eric Severeid

☐ **A Supposedly Fun Thing I'll Never Do Again: Essays and Arguments,** David Foster Wallace

☐ **At My French Table: Food, Family, and Joie de Vivre in a Corner of Normandy,** Jane Webster

☐ **Seeing is Forgetting the Name of the Thing One Sees: A Life of Contemporary Artist Robert Irwin,** Lawrence Weschler

☐ **Stoner,** John Williams

☐ **WPA Guide to Minnesota**

☐ **Above the River: The Complete Poems,** James Wright

☐ **The Book Thief,** Markus Zusak

Let the Great World Spin, Colum McCann

Set mainly in New York in the seventies, this novel explores what else might have happened the day Philippe Petit walked a tightrope between the twin towers. Colum McCann is, in my mind, one of our greatest living writers. This one is just chock full of gorgeous moments. Every page has a sentence that'll knock your socks off.

Canoeing with the Cree, Eric Severeid

The story of two teenagers who canoe from Minneapolis to the Hudson Bay. One of my more memorable reading experiences ever. If you have a beating heart, you will love this book.

Seeing Is Forgetting the Name of the Thing One Sees: A Life of Contemporary Artist Robert Irwin, Lawrence Weschler

A conversation between two men absolutely brimming with curiosity. Weschler's interviews with light/space artist Robert Irwin delve into the ways we as humans experience art.

Maria's Bookshop

DURANGO, CO

Maria's Bookshop has been a full-service general bookstore since 1984, sponsoring over a hundred local reading groups and hosting dozens of special events a year. Included on the Sustainable Business List compiled by Fort Lewis College's Environmental Center, Maria's Bookshop has purchased 100 percent wind power, buys supplies from independent local businesses, reuses or recycles all packaging, and even provides monthly gift certificates to a local shoe or bike shop for employees who walk, bike, or take public transportation to work.

Strongly committed to community, Maria's Bookshop donates to over a hundred community charities and events every year; participates in the American Booksellers Association's Indiebound program, which promotes local, independent businesses; is a founding member of Local First, an independent business alliance in La Plata County; provides free exhibit space for local artists; and devotes significant shelf space to green and community health–themed publications.

www.mariasbookshop.com

LIBBY COWLES,
COMMUNITY RELATIONS MANAGER

What is one thing about bookselling most people don't know?

It requires a genuine appreciation of people. No misanthrope will survive long working at a bookshop (unless, perhaps, that's the vibe that particular store is going for . . .). We're book nerds, yes, but we're also community members and your neighbors, who love seeing people from all walks of life come through our doors with the glint in their eyes that says, "I am ready for my next read—help me find it."

What would be book number 51 on your list?

In *Say Her Name,* Francisco Goldman mines the unbearable loss of his impish, vibrant, brilliant young wife, Aura, through the painstaking excavation of their love and marriage, all the while questioning his complicity in her death. A rumination on grief, but, more fully and accurately, a tenderly drawn, devoted celebration of the ways in which passionate, adult, intellectual, and artistic love emboldens and enriches life. This book is, simply put, stunning.

What book is on your nightstand right now?

In One Person, by John Irving; *West of Here,* by Jonathan Evison; *Contents May Have Shifted,* by Pam Houston; and *Tintin: Destination Moon,* by Herge (but only because my nine-year-old was reading in my room yesterday).

LIBBY'S LIST

- [ ] **A Natural History of Love,** Diane Ackerman
- [ ] **One Hundred Names for Love: A Stroke, a Marriage, and the Language of Healing,** Diane Ackerman
- [ ] **The Lone Ranger and Tonto Fistfight in Heaven,** Sherman Alexie
- [ ] **How the Garcia Girls Lost Their Accents,** Julia Alvarez
- [ ] **Bless Me, Ultima,** Rudolfo Anaya
- [ ] **The Handmaid's Tale,** Margaret Atwood
- [ ] **Women's Ways of Knowing: The Development of Self, Voice, and Mind,** Mary Belenkey et al.
- [ ] **Claiming Ground,** Laura Bell
- [ ] **How to Cook Everything: 2,000 Simple Recipes for Great Food,** Mark Bittman
- [ ] **America America,** Ethan Canin
- [ ] **Yellowcake,** Ann Cummins
- [ ] **Charlie and the Chocolate Factory,** Roald Dahl
- [ ] **Ingri and Edgar Parin D'Aulaire's Book of Greek Myths**
- [ ] **A Heartbreaking Work of Staggering Genius,** Dave Eggers
- [ ] **Ex Libris: Confessions of a Common Reader,** Anne Fadiman
- [ ] **The Great Gatsby,** F. Scott Fitzgerald

- [ ] **Harriet the Spy,** Louise Fitzhugh
- [ ] **Pedagogy of the Oppressed,** Paulo Freire
- [ ] **Dreaming in Cuban,** Cristina Garcia
- [ ] **My Side of the Mountain,** Jean Craighead George
- [ ] **In a Different Voice: Psychological Theory and Women's Development,** Carol Gilligan
- [ ] **The Yellow Wallpaper,** Charlotte Perkins Gilman
- [ ] **Howl and Other Poems,** Allen Ginsberg
- [ ] **Writing Down the Bones: Freeing the Writer Within,** Natalie Goldberg
- [ ] **The Confessions of Max Tivoli,** Andrew Sean Greer
- [ ] **Anthropology of an American Girl,** Hilary Thayer Hamann
- [ ] **The Bone People,** Keri Hulme
- [ ] **Their Eyes Were Watching God,** Zora Neale Hurston
- [ ] **Gnomes,** Will Huygen
- [ ] **The Phantom Tollbooth,** Norton Juster
- [ ] **The Dharma Bums,** Jack Kerouac
- [ ] **A Separate Peace,** John Knowles
- [ ] **Into the Wild,** Jon Krakauer
- [ ] **Woodswoman: Living Alone in the Adirondack Wilderness,** Anne LaBastille
- [ ] **Operating Instructions: A Journal of My Son's First Year,** Anne Lamott

- [ ] **Last Child in the Woods: Saving Our Children from Nature-Deficit Disorder,** Richard Louv
- [ ] **The Emperor's Children,** Claire Messud
- [ ] **A Gate at the Stairs,** Lorrie Moore
- [ ] **The Bluest Eye,** Toni Morrison
- [ ] **Dream Work,** Mary Oliver
- [ ] **Special Topics in Calamity Physics,** Marisha Pessl
- [ ] **Reviving Ophelia: Saving the Selves of Adolescent Girls,** Mary Pipher
- [ ] **Catcher in the Rye,** J. D. Salinger
- [ ] **The Grapes of Wrath,** John Steinbeck
- [ ] **Walden,** Henry David Thoreau
- [ ] **The Lonely Polygamist,** Brady Udall
- [ ] **The Beauty Myth: How Images of Beauty Are Used against Women,** Naomi Wolf
- [ ] **Revolutionary Road,** Richard Yates
- [ ] **Owl Moon,** Jane Yolen
- [ ] **A People's History of the United States,** Howard Zinn

Ex Libris: Confessions of a Common Reader,
Anne Fadiman

This is truly a biliophile's book, and I love it most for the beautiful essay "Marrying Libraries," in which she excavates the deeply considered and heavily loaded decision-making that goes into combining two avid readers' gargantuan book collections.

The Bone People, Keri Hulme

I have never come across a character who has haunted me more than Hulme's fierce protagonist. Even after all these years, I can feel Kerewin's fragile strength and visualize her tower of a home. Simon, the mysterious mute boy whose life randomly intersects with hers, is equally memorable. I can't stop recommending this one.

The Phantom Tollbooth, Norton Juster

The book that made me love language. There's nothing more clever or pun-ridden out there.

The Lonely Polygamist, Brady Udall

I never imagined I'd feel such sympathy for Golden Richards, the husband of four wives and father to twenty-eight children who falls for his boss's wife while building a whorehouse in the Nevada desert. Hilarious, engrossing, and entertaining, Udall's novel is ultimately the story of just another slightly dysfunctional American family trying to balance work, parenting, love, and financial survival. A John Irving for the West.

Prairie Lights Books

IOWA CITY, IA

First opening its doors in 1978, Prairie Lights has three-and-a-half floors containing a bookstore, the Times Club Café, and a gallery space. The café is located in the space where a local literary society met in the thirties, hosting writers Carl Sandburg, Robert Frost, Sherwood Anderson, Langston Hughes, e e cummings, and others. Live from Prairie Lights is an internationally known readings series that features some of the best up-and-coming and well-established authors and poets from around the world. Presented before a live audience and streamed over the internet, this long-running series brings the spoken word from the bookstore to the world at large.

www. prairielights.com

PAUL INGRAM, BOOK BUYER

How did you become a bookseller?

I became a bookseller, as far as I can tell, because I grew up a small, undersocialized kid no one would play with. My father read me *Treasure Island,* to my delight. At thirteen I found a copy of Maugham's *Of Human Bondage* around the house and read it in a few days. Philip Carey's poignant journey showed me how deeply moving a novel could be. My father brought home books he thought I'd like—*Catcher in the Rye,* which thrilled me; *The Big Sky,* by A. B. Guthrie.

The high school library provided friends. *A Tree Grows in Brooklyn,* which I still read every couple of years; *My Ántonia,* which made me cry in that wonderful good read kind of cry. It remains on my list of rereadables. I became less lonely. I began to find other kids who grew experience from between the pages of good books. We shared.

I knew of libraries, but no bookstores. My first bookstore was Discount Books in Washington, DC. They arranged their books by publisher, I'll never know why. I was aghast at the number of books and swore I'd never live anywhere too far from such a place again.

All my grown-up jobs have been at bookstores. Where else might one want to work? It was toward the end of my career that I realized I was dooming myself to poverty. I am proud to be a bookseller, and have come to realize that there are worse things than being broke—*Down and Out in Paris and London,* anyone?

PAUL'S LIST

☐ **A Death in the Family,** James Agee

☐ **The Man with the Golden Arm,** Nelson Algren

☐ **The Mercy Seat,** Rilla Askew

☐ **The Handmaid's Tale,** Margaret Atwood

☐ **A Long Long Way,** Sebastian Barry

☐ **Observatory Mansions,** Edward Carey

☐ **My Ántonia,** Willa Cather

☐ **The Gift of Stones,** Jim Crace

☐ **The Deptford Trilogy,** Robertson Davies

☐ **The Pickwick Papers,** Charles Dickens

☐ **The Living,** Annie Dillard

☐ **Stones for Ibarra,** Harriet Doerr

☐ **The Book of Ebenezer Le Page,** G. B. Edwards

☐ **Absalom, Absalom!,** William Faulkner

☐ **The Unvanquished,** William Faulkner

☐ **Sarah Canary,** Karen Joy Fowler

☐ **Old Filth,** Jane Gardam

☐ **The White Bone,** Barbara Gowdy

☐ **The Tin Drum,** Gunter Grass

☐ **When Madeline Was Young,** Jane Hamilton

- [ ] **The Tie That Binds,** Kent Haruf
- [ ] **Do the Windows Open?,** Julie Hecht
- [ ] **The Friends of Eddie Coyle,** George V. Higgins
- [ ] **Riddley Walker,** Russell Hoban
- [ ] **The Colony of Unrequited Dreams,** Wayne Johnston
- [ ] **The Hamilton Case,** Michelle de Kretser
- [ ] **So Long, See You Tomorrow,** William Maxwell
- [ ] **Time Will Darken It,** William Maxwell
- [ ] **Moby-Dick,** Herman Melville
- [ ] **The Heart is a Lonely Hunter,** Carson McCullers
- [ ] **Fugitive Pieces,** Anne Michaels
- [ ] **The Emigrants,** Vilhelm Moberg
- [ ] **Plains Song: For Female Voices,** Wright Morris
- [ ] **Into the Heart of Borneo,** Redmond O'Hanlon
- [ ] **1984,** George Orwell
- [ ] **The Moviegoer,** Walker Percy
- [ ] **Masters of Atlantis,** Charles Portis
- [ ] **True Grit,** Charles Portis
- [ ] **Home,** Marilynne Robinson
- [ ] **Housekeeping,** Marilynne Robinson
- [ ] **A Blessing on the Moon,** Joseph Skibell
- [ ] **A Tree Grows in Brooklyn,** Betty Smith
- [ ] **The Afterlife of George Cartwright,** John Steffler

- [ ] **The Far Euphrates,** Aryeh Lev Stollman
- [ ] **The Blackwater Lightship,** Colm Toibin
- [ ] **Music and Silence,** Rose Tremain
- [ ] **The Story of Lucy Gault,** Willaim Trevor
- [ ] **The Collected Stories of Eudora Welty**
- [ ] **The Intuitionist,** Colson Whitehead
- [ ] **Clara Callan,** Richard B. Wright

I love novels that come at me out of the blue, mysterious authors attempting things fresh and strange, which have an appeal I can't explain. Jim Crace, author of *Gift of Stones,* had the vision to write a novel set in a Neolithic Europe. The main character is a young boy who loses an arm and must find a way for himself in a world that makes stone tools with two arms. "It has no basis in reality," Crace once told me. "I made up everything." A beautiful book.

I also like certain editors and watch for their work. Chip Fleischer at Steerforth has published great stuff. Castle Freeman Jr.'s *Go With Me** is a tight, perfectly shaped little novel set deep in the wilds of Vermont among baddies and people who want to be left alone. A woman leads two men to hunt down a tormentor. A handful of old farts acts as a Greek chorus. I just keep reading it. The author works on the *Old Farmer's Almanac.*

Michelle de Kretser is a Sinhalese novelist writing and teaching in Australia. *The Hamilton Case* (sounds like a Perry Mason episode) takes a look at the twentieth century through the eyes of a Eurasian lawyer who would like nothing more than for the English to accept him as English. They will not. It is a book of carefully constructed, deeply ironic sentences that shine brightly, shift gears, and invite rereading. It is a tragicomedy of English colonialism, the plot of which hinges on the outcome of a legal case. My highest-end mystery customers think it's the top of the top.

*not on Paul's list, but still a firm favorite of his

Rakestraw Books

DANVILLE, CA

Established in 1973, Rakestraw Books is one of the Bay Area's premier venues for author readings and signings. As a literary community center, Rakestraw Books has been an active philanthropist over the years, donating cash and in-kind donations of gift certificates, books, specially created author visits, and rare signed first editions for charity auctions and fundraisers. Rakestraw Books also hosts special events benefiting nonprofit organizations, particularly those that support literacy, reading, and the arts. Its First Editions Club allows members to receive a signed first edition of books by both established and emerging writers.

www.rakestrawbooks.com

MICHAEL BARNARD,
OWNER AND PRESIDENT

What book is on your nightstand right now?

Five books, three of which are part of long-term resolutions. The first is *Swann's Way,* by Marcel Proust (translated by Lydia Davis). I'm trying to read ten pages a day till I've read all six volumes. It's grander and more engaging and quite a bit more difficult than I expected. I'm also trying to read two poems a day, so I have my grandfather's old copy of *The Oxford Book of English Verse*, edited by Sir Arthur Quiller-Couch, and Wendell Berry's *Window Poems*. I am finding that reading poetry slows me down while also focusing my thinking. It's deeply refreshing. I also have two advance reading copies: *Canada,* by Richard Ford, and *Why Be Happy When You Could Be Normal?* by Jeannette Winterson. Each has such a distinctive and powerful voice but each is grappling with the same questions: Why are we here? What is the nature of life?

What is your favorite bookstore (besides the one you work at)?

In thinking of all the shops that I have loved and admired, I return again and again to City Lights Books in San Francisco and, at least in memory, to an old paperback used bookstore called Hooked on Books in Walnut Creek, California. The merits and charms of City Lights are many and varied: its sense of place, its historic role, and its informed curatorial viewpoint. It is so completely and marvelously itself. The old Hooked on Books may have been little different from most suburban used bookstores of its time, but I have known no store so deeply or over such a long period of time. Whether it was discovering Enid Blyton's Famous Five novels in the children's section to reading Voltaire's *Candide* while sitting in the classics room during one rainy afternoon, the books I bought there shaped my life. That perfectly ordinary and perfectly wonderful shop was the escape hatch that opened up the world for me. I love its memory still and miss it.

MICHAEL'S LIST

- [ ] **Pride and Prejudice,** Jane Austen
- [ ] **The Ninemile Wolves,** Rick Bass
- [ ] **Mapp and Lucia,** E. F. Benson
- [ ] **The Weekend,** Peter Cameron
- [ ] **The Amazing Adventures of Kavalier and Clay,** Michael Chabon
- [ ] **Jonathan Strange & Mr. Norrell,** Susanna Clarke
- [ ] **Miss Rumphius,** Barbara Cooney
- [ ] **A Home at the End of the World,** Michael Cunningham
- [ ] **The Decline and Fall of Practically Everybody: Great Figures of History Hilariously Humbled,** Will Cuppy
- [ ] **What's Bred in the Bone,** Robertson Davies
- [ ] **Cabal,** Michael Dibdin
- [ ] **Bleak House,** Charles Dickens
- [ ] **Zeitoun,** Dave Eggers
- [ ] **Then There Were Five,** Elizabeth Enright
- [ ] **West of Here,** Jonathan Evison
- [ ] **A Time of Gifts: On Foot to Constantinople: From the Hook of Holland to the Middle Danube,** Patrick Leigh Fermor
- [ ] **The Gastronomical Me,** M. F. K. Fisher
- [ ] **A Room with a View,** E. M. Forster

- [ ] **Neverwhere,** Neil Gaiman
- [ ] **Of Love and Other Demons,** Gabriel Garcia Márquez
- [ ] **Three Junes,** Julia Glass
- [ ] **Comfort and Joy,** Jim Grimsley
- [ ] **The Magicians,** Lev Grossman
- [ ] **The Art of Fielding,** Chad Harbach
- [ ] **A Portrait of the Artist as a Young Man,** James Joyce
- [ ] **The Phantom Tollbooth,** Norton Juster
- [ ] **The Gammage Cup: A Novel of the Minnipins,** Carol Kendall
- [ ] **The Dharma Bums,** Jack Kerouac
- [ ] **Ship of Gold in the Deep Blue Sea: The History and Discovery of the World's Richest Shipwreck,** Gary Kinder
- [ ] **King Matt the First,** Janusz Korczak
- [ ] **A Wizard of Earthsea,** Ursula K. Le Guin
- [ ] **Danube,** Patrick Leigh Fermor
- [ ] **Between Meals: An Appetite for Paris,** A. J. Liebling
- [ ] **Tales of the City,** Armistead Maupin
- [ ] **The Bottom of the Harbor,** Joseph Mitchell
- [ ] **The Blessing,** Nancy Mitford
- [ ] **The Lonely Passion of Judith Hearne,** Brian Moore
- [ ] **Last Letters from Hav,** Jan Morris

- [ ] **The Rape of Europa: The Fate of Europe's Treasures in the Third Reich and the Second World War,** Lynn H. Nicholas

- [ ] **The Queen of the South,** Arturo Pérez-Reverte

- [ ] **Close Range: Wyoming Stories,** Annie Proulx

- [ ] **The Amber Spyglass,** Philip Pullman

- [ ] **Quartet in Autumn,** Barbara Pym

- [ ] **Haroun and the Sea of Stories,** Salman Rushdie

- [ ] **The Guernsey Literary and Potato Peel Pie Society,** Mary Ann Schaffer and Annie Barrows

- [ ] **White Teeth,** Zadie Smith

- [ ] **Rip-Rap and Cold Mountain Poems,** Gary Snyder

- [ ] **The Prime of Miss Jean Brodie,** Muriel Spark

- [ ] **The Franchise Affair,** Josephine Tey

- [ ] **The Leopard,** Giuseppe Tomasi di Lampedusa

- [ ] **A Boy's Own Story,** Edmund White

Then There Were Five, Elizabeth Enright

This is first book I ever ordered from a used bookstore—the old Holmes Book Company in Oakland—and still one of my all-time favorite summertime stories: excitement, friendship, and a chapter-long riff on the joys of canning!

A Time of Gifts: On Foot to Constantinople: From the Hook of Holland to the Middle Danube,
Patrick Leigh Fermor

When I was nineteen years old, I wanted to be Paddy Fermor: he was worldly, terribly well-read, and so sexy that the Mitford sisters' nickname for him was "The Body." Plus, he was the inspiration for James Bond. This account of the first part of his youthful trek from Holland to Constantinople is one of the best travelogues ever written.

The Leopard, Giuseppe Tomasi di Lampedusa

I've heard it characterized as an Italian *Gone with the Wind,* but to me this sweeping, romantic, and tragic novel is so much more. It is suffused with that perfect golden late-afternoon light that is the color of nostalgia and unfillable longing.

Last Letters from Hav, Jan Morris

The fictional city of Hav becomes the central character in Jan Morris's unusual only novel. Revolutionaries, socialites, and mystics all passed through Hav and left their mark on this mysterious city somewhere in the Near East.

Quartet in Autumn, Barbara Pym

I spent my junior year of college in Scotland. During that Wunderjahr, my mother sent me a care package including Pym's beautiful, haunting, and unforgettable novel. It's out of print but worth seeking out.

The Regulator Bookshop

DURHAM, NC

As the founding member of "Sustain-a-Bull: Shop Independent Durham," the Regulator Bookshop (regulatorbookshop.com) is at the heart of Durham's shop local movement. A vital cultural hub of the community for more than thirty-five years, the Regulator brings together readers, authors, town, and gown.

When the Regulator first opened for business on December 4, 1976, the store arranged for its first customer to be Agnes Birkhead—the court stenographer at the Scopes Monkey Trial and later personal assistant to Sinclair Lewis (and the grandmother of one of the store's founders). For the Regulator, Agnes Birkhead was a connection to a strong American tradition of truth seeking and independent thinking—a tradition the store strives to continue.

www.sustainabull.net

TOM CAMPBELL, CO-OWNER

Which book on your list do you think is particularly underrated?

A collection of short stories, *The Country of the Pointed Firs,* by Sarah Orne Jewett, depicts the often-isolated lives of a group of strong women living in coastal Maine in the late nineteenth century. Shot through with the thin clear light of a Maine spring day, the stories portray these women with an appreciation that borders on reverence. *The Country of the Pointed Firs* is easily a match for Willa Cather's best writing.

Who is your most trusted source for book recommendations?

There are a small handful of friends, customers, and coworkers whose book recommendations I have come to trust. As far as I can tell the only other thing these folks have in common is that they read a lot. But if you know someone whose taste in reading parallels yours, here is a good thing to try: Get a recommendation from your friend of a book you haven't heard of. Make sure your friend tells you only the title and author. Buy the book without reading any of the descriptions or blurbs on the book's cover (it can help to immediately wrap the book in a plain new cover). Then read the book without knowing anything about it. Then it's just you and the story, pure and simple.

TOM'S LIST

- [ ] **Bottom of the 33rd: Hope, Redemption, and Baseball's Longest Game,** Dan Barry
- [ ] **Any Human Heart,** William Boyd
- [ ] **Ethel and Ernest: A True Story,** Raymond Briggs
- [ ] **Possession,** A. S. Byatt
- [ ] **The Big Sleep,** Raymond Chandler
- [ ] **Little, Big,** John Crowley
- [ ] **Sherlock Holmes: The Complete Novels and Stories,** Arthur Conan Doyle
- [ ] **At Day's Close: Night in Times Past,** A. Roger Ekirch
- [ ] **Birdsong: A Novel of Love and War,** Sebastian Faulks
- [ ] **A Time of Gifts: On Foot to Constantinople: From the Hook of Holland to the Middle Danube,** Patrick Leigh Fermor
- [ ] **The Great Gatsby,** F. Scott Fitzgerald
- [ ] **The Lay of the Land,** Richard Ford
- [ ] **Not Your Usual Founding Father: Selected Readings from Benjamin Franklin**
- [ ] **Cold Mountain,** Charles Frazier
- [ ] **Death of the Fox: A Novel of Elizabeth and Raleigh,** George Garrett
- [ ] **Last Train to Memphis: The Rise of Elvis Presley,** Peter Guralnick

- ☐ **The Curious Incident of the Dog in the Night-Time,** Mark Haddon
- ☐ **The Raw Shark Texts,** Steven Hall
- ☐ **The Heart of Understanding: Commentaries on the Prajnaparamita Heart Sutra,** Thich Nhat Hanh
- ☐ **Catch-22,** Joseph Heller
- ☐ **A Farewell to Arms,** Ernest Hemingway
- ☐ **Dispatches,** Michael Herr
- ☐ **The Country of the Pointed Firs and Other Stories,** Sarah Orne Jewett
- ☐ **Motherless Brooklyn,** Jonathan Lethem
- ☐ **Oak: The Frame of Civilization,** William Bryant Logan
- ☐ **Island: The Complete Stories,** Alistair MacLeod
- ☐ **Love in the Time of Cholera,** Gabriel Garcia Márquez
- ☐ **The Snow Leopard,** Peter Matthiessen
- ☐ **Let the Great World Spin,** Colum McCann
- ☐ **Angela's Ashes,** Frank McCourt
- ☐ **Charming Billy,** Alice McDermott
- ☐ **On Food and Cooking: The Science and Lore of the Kitchen,** Harold McGee
- ☐ **If Nobody Speaks of Remarkable Things,** Jon McGregor
- ☐ **Up in the Old Hotel,** Joseph Mitchell
- ☐ **Eating the Sun: How Plants Power the Planet,** Oliver Morton

- [ ] **Aubrey/Maturin novels,** Patrick O'Brian
- [ ] **Trawler: A Journey Through the North Atlantic,** Redmond O'Hanlon
- [ ] **Citizens of London: The Americans Who Stood with Britain in Its Darkest, Finest Hour,** Lynne Olson
- [ ] **The Collected Essays, Journalism and Letters of George Orwell**
- [ ] **The Glory of Their Times: The Story of the Early Days of Baseball Told by the Men Who Played It,** Lawrence S. Ritter
- [ ] **A Sport and a Pastime,** James Salter
- [ ] **Balzac and the Little Chinese Seamstress,** Dai Sijie
- [ ] **Last Orders,** Graham Swift
- [ ] **Arabian Sands,** Wilfred Thesiger
- [ ] **The Lord of the Rings,** J. R. R. Tolkien
- [ ] **War and Peace,** Leo Tolstoy
- [ ] **The Miracle Life of Edgar Mint,** Brady Udall
- [ ] **Morality Play,** Barry Unsworth
- [ ] **Cutting for Stone,** Abraham Verghese
- [ ] **The Intuitionist,** Colson Whitehead

The Raw Shark Texts, Steven Hall

Looking at the fiction on my list, it's clear I have a soft spot for the well-told sentimental story. So I figured I needed a book or two that cut against my sentimental side. Enter *The Raw Shark Texts*. The shark is out there. Attacking people. Eating them. But wait—the shark here is a conceptual shark. It eats people's identities. Their concept of themselves, if you will. Our hero, determined to reclaim his identity and a lost love, goes on a shark hunt, and suddenly the game's afoot!

The Raw Shark Texts is great fun. Smart, edgy, and with a plot that gets you into the chase yourself. A *Jaws,* or maybe a *Moby-Dick,* for our postmodern times.

Dispatches, Michael Herr

Thirty years after I first read it, I still remember, word for word, the first sentence of Michael Herr's *Dispatches:* "Going out at night the medics gave you pills, Dexedrine breath like dead snakes kept too long in a jar."

"Dexedrine breath like dead snakes kept too long in a jar"—Where could that amazing image have come from? Who among us has ever actually smelled dead snakes kept too long in a jar? Yet we know exactly what Michael Herr is talking about.

Michael Herr was a reporter covering the war in Vietnam. Today we would say he was embedded with the troops. *Dispatches* is a great book—with moments of pure brilliance—about the on-the-ground experience of Vietnam.

RiverRun Bookstore

PORTSMOUTH, NH

RiverRun Bookstore opened their doors in 2002. They sell new and used books with an emphasis on fiction, history, poetry, and mystery. RiverRun hosts more than 150 events a year and has a signed first editions club. In their own words, "We are living the dream! No, really, we are. People always say 'I've always wanted to open a bookstore' with a wistful look, like they would have done it if only they had drawn the lucky number, or found the golden ticket. Or they would have done it if it wasn't a completely crazy, quixotic endeavor in this modern world. Well we did it, and all it took was guts, and faith in our community."

www.riverrunbookstore.com

Who is your most trusted source for book recommendations?
Working in a bookstore, I discover so many books all the time. But I also love getting recommendations from like-minded book lovers. And my neighbor's dog. One of these things is true.

What's the oddest book request or question you've received from a customer?
"Did Stieg Larsson write the *Girl with the Dragon Tattoo* series before he died?"

What do you think is a particularly underrated book on your list?
So many of them, but that's what's great about hand-selling: You can say, "So you read (insert best-selling book that practically everyone on the planet has read) and loved it. Now, here's a really spectacular book that you may not have heard about that you're going to love, too. Trust me—I'm a professional."

What book is on your nightstand now?
I have over nine hundred unread books in my house—I am an unapologetic biblioholic. I end up buying at least one book every time I work. (My boss is a very wise man.) It's exciting, finishing a book, and then going to my

shelves to choose the next one. It's like having a bookstore in my house. Except you're not required to wear pants.

What is your favorite bookstore (besides the one you work at)?
Any independent bookstore out there has my love. They're all beautiful.

- ☐ **The Plague Dogs,** Richard Adams
- ☐ **Wintergirls,** Laurie Halse Anderson
- ☐ **Cat's Eye,** Margaret Atwood
- ☐ **The Wasp Factory,** Iain Banks
- ☐ **The Vaults,** Toby Ball
- ☐ **The Brief History of the Dead,** Kevin Brockmeier
- ☐ **In Cold Blood,** Truman Capote
- ☐ **Close to Shore: The Terrifying Shark Attacks of 1916,** Michael Capuzzo
- ☐ **One Bloody Thing After Another,** Joey Comeau
- ☐ **Fifth Business,** Robertson Davies
- ☐ **Bad Marie,** Marcy Dermansky
- ☐ **Geek Love,** Katherine Dunn
- ☐ **Zeroville,** Steve Erickson
- ☐ **The Sorrows of a Young Werther,** Johann Wolfgang von Goethe
- ☐ **The Lost City of Z: A Tale of Deadly Obsession in the Amazon,** David Grann
- ☐ **Claire DeWitt and the City of the Dead,** Sara Gran
- ☐ **The Forever War,** Joe Haldeman
- ☐ **The Gone-Away World,** Nick Harkaway

- [ ] **Union Atlantic,** Adam Haslett
- [ ] **Winter's Tale,** Mark Helprin
- [ ] **Rat Girl,** Kristen Hersh
- [ ] **Heart-Shaped Box,** Joe Hill
- [ ] **A High Wind in Jamaica,** Richard Hughes
- [ ] **We Have Always Lived in the Castle,** Shirley Jackson
- [ ] **The Known World,** Edward P. Jones
- [ ] **Mister Pip,** Lloyd Jones
- [ ] **The Dust of 100 Dogs,** A. S. King
- [ ] **Father of the Rain,** Lily King
- [ ] **The Orange Eats Creeps,** Grace Krilanovich
- [ ] **Disquiet,** Julia Leigh
- [ ] **As She Climbed Across the Table,** Jonathan Lethem
- [ ] **Let the Great World Spin,** Colum McCann
- [ ] **Blood Meridian, or the Evening Redness in the West,** Cormac McCarthy
- [ ] **Lonesome Dove,** Larry McMurtry
- [ ] **Cloud Atlas,** David Mitchell
- [ ] **Skippy Dies,** Paul Murray
- [ ] **A Good Man Is Hard to Find and Other Stories,** Flannery O'Connor
- [ ] **Bel Canto,** Ann Patchett
- [ ] **My Name is Asher Lev,** Chaim Potok

- [ ] **Jamestown,** Matthew Sharpe
- [ ] **In Harm's Way: The Sinking of the U.S.S. *Indianapolis* and the Extraordinary Story of Its Survivors,** Doug Stanton
- [ ] **Cannery Row,** John Steinbeck
- [ ] **Anathem,** Neal Stephenson
- [ ] **Perfume: The Story of a Murderer,** Patrick Suskind
- [ ] **The Secret History,** Donna Tartt
- [ ] **The Tiger: A True Story of Vengeance and Survival,** John Vaillant
- [ ] **Zazen,** Vanessa Veselka
- [ ] **Slapstick, or Lonesome No More!,** Kurt Vonnegut
- [ ] **The Little Stranger,** Sarah Waters
- [ ] **The Monstrumologist,** Richard Yancey

The Vaults, Toby Ball
The Vaults kicks off Toby Ball's fantastic City mystery trilogy.

One Bloody Thing After Another, Joey Comeau
One Bloody Thing After Another is fun and gross and sweet, and Joey is awesome.

Claire DeWitt and the City of the Dead, Sara Gran
I love Sara Gran's books so much I just drooled a little on the keyboard typing that.

Zazen, Vanessa Veselka
The Orange Eats Creeps, Grace Krilanovich
Zazen and *The Orange Eats Creeps* are head-explodey, futuristic brilliance that will give you whiplash. In a good way.

Sherman's Books and Stationery

FREEPORT, ME

Maine's oldest bookstore, Sherman's Books and Stationery opened in 1886 in Bar Harbor, Maine, when William Sherman set up a storefront printing press, printing the local newspaper and jobs for residents and summer visitors. With stores in Freeport, Bar Harbor, Camden, and Boothbay Harbor, Sherman's Books and Stationery now provides a full-range bookstore experience, including an extensive collection of books about Maine, Maine stationery, gifts, and toys.

www.shermans.com

JOSH CHRISTIE, BOOKSELLER

What book is on your nightstand right now?
Crogan's Loyalty, the third book in Chris Schweizer's epic Crogan Adventures series for Oni Press.

What's one thing about bookselling most people don't know?
There's an overwhelming sense that a bookstore is like that record store in *High Fidelity;* booksellers hang out, read all day, and talk about books. Unfortunately we only really get to read books on our own time, just like everyone else.

The raw animal magnetism of booksellers, on the other hand, is well documented.

Who is your most trusted source for book recommendations?
Mostly other booksellers (especially the savants at WORD Brooklyn), though we do have a few customers that keep me on my toes with unexpected stuff.

What is your favorite bookstore (besides the one you work at)?
Northshire Books in Manchester Center, Vermont. It's a couple floors of awesome independent bookselling.

Which book on your list do you think is particularly underrated?

The Ridiculous Race, by Steve Hely and Vali Chandrasekaran. It's not a great work of literary art—it's about two comedy writers racing each other around the globe, sans air travel—but it's a hell of a lot of fun. It kind of came out and disappeared in 2008, but it's remained a perennial bestseller (and a favorite hand sell) at our store.

JOSH'S LIST

- [ ] **Speaking Freely: Trials of the First Amendment,** Floyd Abrams

- [ ] **I Found This Funny: My Favorite Pieces of Humor and Some That May Not Be Funny At All,** Judd Apatow

- [ ] **Actual Air,** David Berman

- [ ] **Extra Lives: Why Video Games Matter,** Tom Bissell

- [ ] **The House of Tomorrow,** Peter Bognanni

- [ ] **The Ascent of Rum Doodle,** W. E. Bowman

- [ ] **Active Liberty: Interpreting Our Democratic Constitution,** Stephen Breyer

- [ ] **World War Z: An Oral History of the Zombie War,** Max Brooks

- [ ] **K Blows Top: A Cold War Comic Interlude Starring Nikita Khrushchev, America's Most Unlikely Tourist,** Peter Carlson

- [ ] **Hard Rain Falling,** Don Carpenter

- [ ] **Plato and a Platypus Walk into a Bar . . . : Understanding Philosophy Through Jokes,** Thomas Cathcart and Daniel Klein

- [ ] **The Amazing Adventures of Kavalier and Clay,** Michael Chabon

- [ ] **The Story of Sugarloaf,** John Christie

- [ ] **This Life Is in Your Hands: One Dream, Sixty Acres, and a Family Undone,** Melissa Coleman

- [ ] **The Sisters Brothers,** Patrick deWitt

- [ ] **The Brief Wondrous Life of Oscar Wao,** Junot Díaz

- [ ] **The Last Werewolf,** Glen Duncan

- [ ] **The Vikings: A History,** Robert Ferguson

- [ ] **All the Way Home: Building a Family in a Falling-Down House,** David Giffels

- [ ] **Phonogram: The Singles Club,** Kieron Gillen and Jamie McKelvie

- [ ] **The Tipping Point: How Little Things Can Make a Big Difference,** Malcolm Gladwell

- [ ] **The Magicians,** Lev Grossman

- [ ] **The Gone-Away World,** Nick Harkaway

- [ ] **The Ridiculous Race,** Steve Hely and Vali Chandrasekaran

- [ ] **The Nightly News,** Jonathan Hickman

- [ ] **In Praise of Slowness: Challenging the Cult of Speed,** Carl Honoré

- [ ] **Johannes Cabal the Necromancer,** Jonathan L. Howard

- [ ] **Guide to Getting It On,** Paul Joannides

- [ ] **In the Garden of Beasts: Love, Terror, and an American Family in Hitler's Berlin,** Erik Larson

- [ ] **Freakonomics: A Rogue Economist Explores the Hidden Side of Everything,** Steven D. Levitt and Stephen J. Dubner

- ☐ **A Fraction of the Whole,** Steve Toltz
- ☐ **I Married You for Happiness,** Lily Tuck
- ☐ **Wednesday Comics**
- ☐ **Local,** Brian Wood and Ryan Kelly
- ☐ **Red, White, and Brew: An American Beer Odyssey,** Brian Yaeger

Extra Lives: Why Video Games Matter, Tom Bissell

For someone who grew up in a world saturated with video games, *Extra Lives* was crucial reading, and in a lot of ways is the first book of it's kind. Bissell explores just what games can and can't accomplish as entertainment, and holds the successes and failures of the form up to other narrative media like film and literature. It's certainly the best book on games—and why they matter—that I've read.

Mr. Peanut, Adam Ross

At many points, *Mr. Peanut* is an uncomfortable read. The book swirls around three main characters: David Pepin, a man who is the prime suspect in his wife's murder, and Hastroll and Sheppard, the two detectives investigating the mysterious circumstances of her death. With this narrative framework in place, *Mr. Peanut* is much more concerned with the minds of these three men, and an examination of the deepest, darkest thoughts men have when in marriages or relationships. The mesmerizing story and fascinating study of love made *Mr. Peanut* impossible to put down.

I Married You for Happiness, Lily Tuck

I poke fun at "literary fiction" by saying that it's three hundred pages where nothing happens, and on the surface Tuck's novel seemed like a perfect example. It's a novel about a woman whose husband has just passed away lying in bed, drinking wine, and remembering their life. But I'm so glad I gave it a chance, because it's an intimate, very real story of a decades-long relationship, full of great insight and beautiful writing.

Skylight Books

LOS ANGELES, CA

Skylight Books has been serving Los Angeles neighbor-hoods since 1996. With a self-described eclectic clientele, Skylight Books offers literary fiction; books on music, art, film, and theatre; Los Angeles regional culture and history; comics and graphic literature; children's books; political theory; and more. They also strive to feature LGBT fiction and nonfiction, and have an extensive curated selection of local and international zines. In addition to hosting book groups and events, Skylight Books recently launched its Friends with Benefits Membership Club. Visitors to Skylight Books might also encounter Franny the cat, the store mascot.

www.skylightbooks.com

Who is your most trusted source for book recommendations?
Honestly? Other booksellers and writers. They will often have something to say about all of the best sellers, and then they will recommend three others you've never heard of but that are just as good (or better). These people are aware of the current literary landscape, and they want to help readers situate themselves in relation to that landscape. It's a beautiful thing.

What makes a bookstore successful in today's world?
I recently had a flash of inspiration as to what my life goal is: to make life more bearable for as many people as possible through books and community. If a store can do that while paying its bills, it will be successful. It must respond to the needs and desires of its customers, it must be aware of the trends that are affecting readers everywhere, and it must educate them as to why a store can't just "sell books as cheaply as Amazon does." A successful bookstore must recognize and capitalize on those aspects of their business that an online retailer cannot replicate, without denying the tools that the Internet provides them with.

What book is on your nightstand right now?
The Big Red Book, by Rumi, translated by Coleman Barks.

Which book on your list do you think is particularly underrated?

Mopus, by Oisin Curran (fiction) and *Odysseus in America,* by Jonathan Shay (nonfiction).

- [ ] **The Jolly Postman: or Other People's Letters,**
  Janet and Allan Ahlberg
- [ ] **I, the Divine: A Novel in First Chapters,**
  Rabih Alameddine
- [ ] **Zoom,** Istvan Banyai
- [ ] **Fun Home: A Family Tragicomic,** Alison Bechdel
- [ ] **The Reapers Are the Angels,** Alden Bell
- [ ] **The Correspondence Artist,** Barbara Browning
- [ ] **The Life and Times of the Thunderbolt Kid,** Bill Bryson
- [ ] **Kindred,** Octavia E. Butler
- [ ] **Nox,** Anne Carson
- [ ] **The Slow Fix,** Ivan E. Coyote
- [ ] **Log of the S.S.** *The Mrs. Unguentine,* Stanley Crawford
- [ ] **Mopus,** Oisin Curran
- [ ] **Matilda,** Roald Dahl
- [ ] **White Noise,** Don DeLillo
- [ ] **Little Brother,** Cory Doctorow
- [ ] **As I Lay Dying,** William Faulkner
- [ ] **Color: A Natural History of the Palette,** Victoria Finlay
- [ ] **Man's Search for Meaning,** Viktor E. Frankl
- [ ] **Mirrors: Stories of Almost Everyone,** Eduardo Galeano

- [ ] **The Westing Game,** Ellen Raskin
- [ ] **Odysseus in America: Combat Trauma and Trials of Homecoming,** Jonathan Shay
- [ ] **The Immortal Life of Henrietta Lacks,** Rebecca Skloot
- [ ] **Hotel World,** Ali Smith
- [ ] **Narration: Four Lectures,** Gertrude Stein
- [ ] **Infinite Jest,** David Foster Wallace
- [ ] **The Ultimate Alphabet,** Mike Wilks
- [ ] **Refuge: An Unnatural History of Family and Place,** Terry Tempest Williams
- [ ] **Let's Talk About Love: A Journey to the End of Taste,** Carl Wilson
- [ ] **Written on the Body,** Jeanette Winterson
- [ ] **The Position,** Meg Wolitzer
- [ ] **Flapper: A Madcap Story of Sex, Style, Celebrity, and the Women Who Made Modern America,** Joshua Zeitz

Mirrors: Stories of Almost Everyone, Eduardo Galeano
Reading his world history in vignettes is like watching life form, cell by cell, civilization by civilization, with sparks of wonder melding with flashes of horror. Much like Howard Zinn, Galeano forces the reader to question the objectivity of history as it is presented to you. But he does it all lyrically and nonlinearly, and somehow still encompassingly and almost mythically. It's hard to explain.

Asterios Polyp, David Mazzucchelli
Asterios Polyp was the first book that showed me just how complex and layered and unique storytelling and character development can be when done in the graphic medium.

Well, Matthew McIntosh
True confessions: I haven't read this book yet. (Are booksellers allowed to admit that?) But I'm sure every store has one like it: a book that ripples through the staff and becomes a store best seller loved and recommended by all, and that most booksellers elsewhere (and the general public) haven't heard of.

The Ultimate Alphabet, Mike Wilks

As a child, this book, more than any about distant and exotic lands, gave me a sense of wonder about just how wide the world is, and how there is always more to know than what you think you know. I'm sad that it's out of print.

Written on the Body, Jeanette Winterson

Of all of my favorite writers, I find Winterson to be the most rereadable.

Square Books

OXFORD, MS

Square Books is located on the historic town square of Oxford, Mississippi, home of the University of Mississippi and many great writers, including William Faulkner, Barry Hannah, Larry Brown, and, for a time, Willie Morris and John Grisham. Square Books has been a general independent bookstore since 1979, operating in three separate buildings about one hundred feet apart: the main store is in a two-story building with a café; Off Square Books is a few doors down and features lifestyle sections such as gardening and cookbooks; and Square Books Jr., the children's bookstore, sits on the east side of the square. Square Books prides itself on its selection of literary fiction, books on the American South and by Southern writers, a large inventory of reduced-price remainders, and its children's section. The store hosts the *Thacker Mountain Radio Show* and more than 150 author events a year. They also offer a subscription program for signed first editions.

www.squarebooks.com

RICHARD HOWORTH (OWNER),
CODY MORRISON (BUYER), AND
LYN ROBERTS (GENERAL MANAGER)

Who is your most trusted source for book recommendations?
LR: Generally speaking, I trust my colleagues to recommend books. Once you know what someone's favorites are, it's easy to recommend comparable books. But the booksellers I work with know my favorites and know me, so they can recommend a title that might not, at first glance, seem compatible. I also trust the recommendations of some friends who work for publishers. My interest might be piqued by book blurbers, but I've learned that even though I might admire an author's work, it does not necessarily follow that I will like what they recommend.

What is one thing about bookselling most people don't know?
RH: How much hard work and, if you will, artful retailing it requires to make selling books at all possible to begin with. For something that appears to be so simple and leisurely, there is real toil and mind-numbing detail. When I began bookselling thirty-four years ago, I thought being a writer would be more difficult. I am fairly sure I was wrong about that.

What book is on your nightstand right now?

CM: There is never just one book on my nightstand. I've always got a stack of books in easy reach, and I usually have several books going at the same time. Currently, there is *History of a Pleasure Seeker,* by Richard Mason; *Into the Silence,* by Wade Davis; *The Second Four Books of Poems,* by W. S Merwin; *What It Was,* by George Pelecanos; *Three Weeks in December,* by Andrea Schulman; and *Why Be Normal When You Can Be Happy?* by Jeanette Winterson. Then in several weeks I'll have a new bunch of titles on the nightstand.

LYN'S LIST

- [ ] **The Brief History of the Dead,** Kevin Brockmeier
- [ ] **The Last Good Kiss,** James Crumley
- [ ] **As I Lay Dying,** William Faulkner
- [ ] **Poachers,** Tom Franklin
- [ ] **Love in the Time of Cholera,** Gabriel Garcia Márquez
- [ ] **Airships,** Barry Hannah
- [ ] **The History of Love,** Nicole Krauss
- [ ] **Border Songs,** Jim Lynch
- [ ] **Atonement,** Ian McEwan
- [ ] **The Things They Carried,** Tim O'Brien
- [ ] **The Moviegoer,** Walker Percy
- [ ] **Wide Sargasso Sea,** Jean Rhys
- [ ] **St. Lucy's Home for Girls Raised by Wolves,** Karen Russell
- [ ] **Waterland,** Graham Swift
- [ ] **The Story of Edgar Sawtelle,** David Wroblewski

Ask any bookseller, actually any book lover, for a list of favorites and you are likely to get a list that would change by the minute. My list of favorites is the same, but there are certain books always present. These are titles that are tied to turning points in my life. I've read *The Moviegoer* by Walker Percy a number of times, but the first time I was in college and it was an awakening for me. After college I planned to move to Oxford, Mississippi, and not having spent time here, was worried that it would be a cultural wasteland. Once I learned that it was the residence of Barry Hannah, the author of *Airships,* an electrifying collection of short stories, I knew my fears were misplaced. Once established in Yoknapatawpha, I had to read more Faulkner and picked up *As I Lay Dying* and realized how very deadpan funny it is. All of these I have read a number of times, and they are not only fresh each time, but better.

RICHARD'S LIST

- [ ] **Father and Son,** Larry Brown
- [ ] **The Pleasures of the Damned: Poems, 1951–1993,** Charles Bukowski
- [ ] **The Marriage Plot,** Jeffrey Eugenides
- [ ] **Erasure,** Percival Everett
- [ ] **Freedom,** Jonathan Fanzen
- [ ] **Selected Short Stories,** William Faulkner
- [ ] **Rock Springs,** Richard Ford
- [ ] **Long, Last, Happy,** Barry Hannah
- [ ] **The English Major,** Jim Harrison
- [ ] **Round Rock,** Michelle Huneven
- [ ] **Resuscitation of a Hanged Man,** Denis Johnson
- [ ] **Lit,** Mary Karr
- [ ] **Comedy in a Minor Key,** Hans Keilson
- [ ] **The Typist,** Michael Knight
- [ ] **A Gate at the Stairs,** Lorrie Moore
- [ ] **Friend of My Youth,** Alice Munro
- [ ] **Music of the Swamp,** Lewis Nordan
- [ ] **Wise Blood,** Flannery O'Connor
- [ ] **All God's Dangers: The Life of Nate Shaw,** Theodore Rosengarten

- [ ] **The Age of Grief,** Jane Smiley
- [ ] **The Adrian Mole Diaries,** Sue Townsend
- [ ] **Salvage the Bones,** Jesmyn Ward
- [ ] **One Writer's Beginnings,** Eudora Welty
- [ ] **The Electric Kool-Aid Acid Test,** Tom Wolfe

Long, Last, Happy (Barry Hannah) is a generous selection of stories by one of the great short story masters of our time, a writer who has steadily held the admiration of writing students for the last four decades.

Music of the Swamp (Lewis Nordan) is a moving and inventive book written in almost magical prose, and is the book that best exemplifies the author's ambition (paraphrased) "to write about love and death in a humorous way."

All God's Dangers (Theodore Rosengarten) is the book I reach for when anyone asks me for "just one book that explains the South."

CODY'S LIST

☐ **The Savage Detectives,** Roberto Bolaño

☐ **Joe,** Larry Brown

☐ **Among the Thugs,** Bill Buford

☐ **Rides of the Midway,** Lee Durkee

☐ **Ninety-two in the Shade,** Thomas McGuane

☐ **Last Days of Summer,** Steve Kluger

☐ **The Tiger's Wife,** Téa Obreht

☐ **The Moviegoer,** Walker Percy

☐ **Balzac and the Little Chinese Seamstress,** Dai Sijie

☐ **The Salt Line,** Elizabeth Spencer

☐ **Dino: Living High in the Dirty Business of Dreams,**
Nick Tosches

☐ **Lean on Pete,** Willy Vlautin

☐ **Last Days of the Dog-Men,** Brad Watson

☐ **Sent for You Yesterday,** John Edgar Wideman

☐ **The Winter of Frankie Machine,** Don Winslow

The Savage Detectives is easily one of my favorite novels of the last decade. Bolaño is a mad genius. Think Borges meets Kerouac meets Raymond Chandler and you begin to get the picture.

The Last Days of Summer (Steve Kluger) is a book that I can't imagine anyone not liking. Set in 1940s Brooklyn, it's about ten-year-old outcast Joey Margolis who is in search of a hero. Joey lands on Charlie Banks, the star third baseman for the New York Giants. Told through letters, postcards, and newspaper clippings the result is a sweet (but not too sweet), hilarious novel with a big heart that will appeal to all ages.

The Winter of Frankie Machine (Don Winslow) is a nearly perfect book. Once when I was laid up sick, I started this novel and despite being on heavy cold meds found that I had read till two in the morning to in order to finish it. Frankie Machine is a bad mother . . .

Subterranean Books

ST. LOUIS, MO

Opening its doors in 2000, Subterranean Books focuses on independent bookstore best sellers, cult classics, quirky small press publications, and timeless literature. Their biggest categories are literature, music, film, pop culture, art, children's books, cultural studies, and history. Their smaller selections include books on religion, crafts, science, nature, cookbooks, gardening, and travel. At Subterranean Books, the entire staff has input on what is stocked, so the store's selection is always evolving. The store also houses an art gallery. They host many literary and arts events, a children's story time, and also have a free frequent buyer program.

www.subbooks.com

KELLY VON PLONSKI, OWNER

What makes a bookstore successful in today's world?
Neighborhood buy-in is the most important component of a bookstore's success. The store's neighbors have to want the store to be there, and it has to be their go-to place for books. Customer service is paramount for a small store. Every person who walks through the door has to feel welcomed. Shoppers can get algorithmic recommendations and indifferent customer service by shopping online. They choose to come to a real store for warmth.

What book is on your nightstand right now?
My current read is Steve Erickson's *These Dreams of You.*

What is your favorite bookstore (besides the one you work at)?
I have a mild obsession with McNally Jackson.

What is one thing about bookselling most people do not know?
So many folks assume we just sit and read all day. I guess I should be happy that maybe we're able to hide our underwear—the straightening, the cleaning, the accounting, etc., and that all they see is the pretty dress.

Who is your most trusted source for book recommendations?
As far as stocking the store, I trust my in-person sales reps. They've spent time in my store and know the types of books we can actually sell. For personal reading, I trust word of mouth. I think that's why shelf talkers are so successful. Customers want to know what books we feel passionately about, and they trust that expertise.

- [ ] **No god but God: The Origins, Evolution, and Future of Islam,** Reza Aslan
- [ ] **The New York Trilogy,** Paul Auster
- [ ] **City of Thieves,** David Benioff
- [ ] **2666,** Roberto Bolaño
- [ ] **Broken Glass Park,** Alina Bronsky
- [ ] **The Children's Book,** A. S. Byatt
- [ ] **An Arsonist's Guide to Writers' Homes in New England,** Brock Clarke
- [ ] **Room,** Emma Donoghue
- [ ] **I Love You, Beth Cooper,** Larry Doyle
- [ ] **Finding Nouf,** Zoë Ferraris
- [ ] **The Eyre Affair,** Jasper Fforde
- [ ] **Time for Bed,** Mem Fox, illustrated by Jane Dyer
- [ ] **Claire DeWitt and the City of the Dead,** Sara Gran
- [ ] **Brighton Rock,** Graham Greene
- [ ] **The Raw Shark Texts,** Steven Hall
- [ ] **Leningrad: State of Siege,** Michael Jones
- [ ] **Library Lion,** Michelle Knudsen, illustrated by Kevin Hawkes
- [ ] **Interpreter of Maladies,** Jhumpa Lahiri

- [ ] **The Selected Works of T. S. Spivet,** Reif Larsen
- [ ] **The Surrendered,** Chang-Rae Lee
- [ ] **The Chronicles of Narnia,** C. S. Lewis
- [ ] **Magic for Beginners,** Kelly Link
- [ ] **The Razor's Edge,** W. Somerset Maugham
- [ ] **Guess How Much I Love You,** Sam McBratney, illustrated by Anita Jeram
- [ ] **Hold Me Closer, Necromancer,** Lish McBride
- [ ] **The Delivery Man,** Joe McGinniss Jr.
- [ ] **A Fine Balance,** Rohinton Mistry
- [ ] **A Dirty Job,** Christopher Moore
- [ ] **Hard-Boiled Wonderland and the End of the World,** Haruki Murakami
- [ ] **Stone's Fall,** Iain Pears
- [ ] **Special Topics in Calamity Physics,** Marisha Pessl
- [ ] **The Little Engine That Could,** Watty Piper
- [ ] **The Omnivore's Dilemma: A Natural History of Four Meals,** Michael Pollan
- [ ] **Wingshooters,** Nina Revoyr
- [ ] **Goodnight, Goodnight, Construction Site,** Sherri Duskey Rinker, illustrated by Tom Lichtenheld
- [ ] **Home** and **Gilead,** Marilynne Robinson
- [ ] **Sergio Makes a Splash,** Edel Rodriguez
- [ ] **The Death Instinct,** Jed Rubenfeld

- ☐ **Nine Stories,** J. D. Salinger
- ☐ **Firmin,** Sam Savage
- ☐ **On Beauty,** Zadie Smith
- ☐ **Kokoro,** Natsume Soseki
- ☐ **The Sociopath Next Door,** Martha Stout
- ☐ **The Getaway,** Jim Thompson
- ☐ **This Is Where I Leave You,** Jonathan Tropper
- ☐ **The Slap,** Christos Tsiolkas
- ☐ **The Lonely Polygamist,** Brady Udall
- ☐ **Voluntary Madness: Lost and Found in the Mental Healthcare System,** Nora Vincent
- ☐ **Shadow of the Wind,** Carlos Ruiz Zafón

City of Thieves, David Benioff
This is such a wonderful story. It's a skilled writer who can weave humor and light into a story set during the Siege of Leningrad. And his storytelling was so compelling that I immediately went in search of nonfiction titles about the siege just to learn more.

I Love You, Beth Cooper, Larry Doyle
This is laugh-out-loud funny. There are scenes that are seared into my memory. It's a great read for everyone—kids, grown-ups, boys, girls.

The Raw Shark Texts, Steven Hall
I have a very hard time explaining this book to folks. I often fall back on, "It's great. Just trust me." This is a fantastic book. It's one of those that makes me think there's a whole lot more going on in there than what I'm grasping . . . but that's O.K. I *never* read books more than once, but this one I would.

Home and **Gilead,** Marilynne Robinson
I always urge folks to read these back to back. They are the same story written from different characters' points of view. Not only is the writing beautiful and the story

engaging, they made me really think about how the same event can be viewed so differently by different people, and that when you think you are saying one thing that the listener may be hearing something else entirely.

The Getaway, Jim Thompson
This is terse, gritty noir. Ignore any film adaptations you've ever seen. The ending is killer.

Tattered Cover Book Store

DENVER, CO

Tattered Cover Book Store began as a small store in 1971 with only 950 square feet of retail space. It now has three expansive locations in the Denver area.

Tattered Cover hosts a variety of reading groups, as well as a journaling group. They run a Rocky Mountain Authors Program through which they sell books by local authors on consignment. Through their Tattered Cover Gives Back program, 1 percent of sales to members are donated to a local nonprofit organization of the member's choice.

www.tatteredcover.com

NEIL STRANDBERG,
FORMER MANAGER OF OPERATIONS*

Which book on your list do you think is particularly underrated?

Being sort of classics-laden (a line of reading I took up only recently when I realized I'm not very clever, accepted being a slow reader, and rejected the expectation of keeping up with new "must reads"), it is hard to argue that much on my list is underrated. Even the stuff that is newer or less popular is well regarded. Instead, I suppose, I'll say that I wish Wodehouse had a wider readership these days. The minute I saw one of those "Who is John Galt?" bumper stickers, I sorely wanted one that said, "Who is Bertie Wooster?" It strikes me that we'd all be better off if we reflected upon our inner Berties, but the reference is too obscure for most motorists in my neighborhood.

Who is your most trusted source for book recommendations?

Nobody, frankly. Not even my colleagues. In fact, I invariably cringe when someone says, "You ought to read this," and I've abandoned book clubs mostly because I can't stand being told what to read (that, and my personality). So, with few exceptions, over the course of my reading life one book has sort of led to another in a progression that is sensible to me but hard to explain or diagram. When I do find myself vexed for what next, I'll thumb through a bunch of stuff, seek reviews or commentary, stream something on Netflix, and, oftentimes, read genre until my mood changes. A huge epiphany that didn't strike for far too long: stop reading what I don't like. Put it down. Stop. No guilt. No regrets.

What is your favorite bookstore (besides the one you work at)?

If you're limiting me to one, how 'bout CityLightsRJ JuliaSquareBooksMcNallyJacksonsandonceuponatime HungryMind.

*Since this was written, Neil has left Tattered Cover and joined the American Booksellers Association.

NEIL'S LIST

- [ ] **The Windup Girl,** Paolo Bacigalupi
- [ ] **The Sot-Weed Factor,** John Barth
- [ ] **True History of the Kelly Gang,** Peter Carey
- [ ] **Farewell, My Lovely,** Raymond Chandler; but I really mean to say all things Chandler
- [ ] **The Worst Journey in the World,** Apsley Cherry-Garrard
- [ ] **Son of the Morning Star: Custer and the Little Bighorn,** Evan S. Connell
- [ ] **The Last of the Mohicans,** James Fenimore Cooper
- [ ] **White Noise,** Don DeLillo
- [ ] **Bleak House,** Charles Dickens
- [ ] **The Count of Monte Cristo,** Alexandre Dumas
- [ ] **The Three Musketeers,** Alexandre Dumas
- [ ] **History of Tom Jones, a Foundling,** Henry Fielding
- [ ] **One Hundred Years of Solitude,** Gabriel Garcia Márquez
- [ ] **The Tin Drum,** Gunter Grass
- [ ] **I, Claudius,** Robert Graves
- [ ] **The Fabric of the Cosmos: Space, Time, and the Texture of Reality,** Brian Greene
- [ ] **Winter's Tale,** Mark Helprin
- [ ] **The Sun Also Rises,** Ernest Hemingway

- [ ] **Dune,** Frank Herbert
- [ ] **The Fatal Shore: The Epic of Australia's Founding,** Robert Hughes
- [ ] **A Prayer for Owen Meany,** John Irving
- [ ] **The Remains of the Day,** Kazuo Ishiguro
- [ ] **Seven Pillars of Wisdom: A Triumph,** T. E. Lawrence
- [ ] **Goodbye, Darkness: A Memoir of the Pacific War,** William Manchester
- [ ] **Blood Meridian, or the Evening Redness in the West,** Cormac McCarthy
- [ ] **Moby-Dick,** Herman Melville
- [ ] **Lolita,** Vladimir Nabakov
- [ ] **Lucifer's Hammer,** Larry Niven and Jerry Pournelle
- [ ] **The Things They Carried,** Tim O'Brien
- [ ] **The English Patient,** Michael Ondaatje
- [ ] **The Omnivore's Dilemma: A Natural History of Four Meals,** Michael Pollan
- [ ] **The Song of the Dodo: Island Biogeography in an Age of Extinction,** David Quammen
- [ ] **The Making of the Atomic Bomb,** Richard Rhodes
- [ ] **Sun of Suns,** Karl Schroeder
- [ ] **The Killer Angels: A Novel of the Civil War,** Michael Shaara
- [ ] **With the Old Breed: At Peleliu and Okinawa,** E. B. Sledge

- [ ] **Gorky Park,** Martin Cruz Smith; but I really mean to say all things Arkady Renko
- [ ] **Longitude: The True Story of a Lone Genius Who Solved the Greatest Scientific Problem of His Time,** Dava Sobel
- [ ] **East of Eden,** John Steinbeck
- [ ] **The Grapes of Wrath,** John Steinbeck
- [ ] **Cryptonomicon,** Neal Stephenson
- [ ] **Snow Crash,** Neal Stephenson
- [ ] **Perfume: The Story of a Murderer,** Patrick Süskind
- [ ] **Vanity Fair,** William Makepeace Thackeray
- [ ] **The Hobbit, or There and Back Again,** J. R. R. Tolkien
- [ ] **The Lord of the Rings,** J. R. R. Tolkien
- [ ] **The Centaur,** John Updike
- [ ] **The Ramayana,** Valmiki (not really "fiction," as such, but one helluva a story)
- [ ] **Naked Economics: Undressing the Dismal Science,** Charles Wheelan
- [ ] **The Code of the Woosters,** P. G. Wodehouse (but I really mean all things Wooster)

The Count of Monte Cristo and **The Three Musketeers,**
Alexandre Dumas

Somewhere along the way—well, not just somewhere: a small midwestern liberal arts college—I got it into my head that all the books by dead white guys were perfectly useless. A history instructor once welled with tears while discussing *Oliver Twist,* and I sneered at him, inwardly. For years, before I learned shame, I would recall the class and sneer all over again, congratulating myself on my sophisticated taste for contemporary world literature.

I will not say that I then grew up, but more recently life's whirligig of joy, horror, disappointment, and surprise demanded a new reading angle. I needed anchoring in something beyond the present moment.

Unexpectedly, I was rescued by *The Three Musketeers,* which I picked up really only because I very much liked the cover of Viking's hardcover Pevear translation. But that was just the start, since afterward came *Count of Monte Cristo* and then Fielding, Hugo, Thackeray, and yes, Professor Itzkowitz, Dickens (not so much *Oliver Twist,* but *David Copperfield*! So much love in that book. I well up . . .).

Perhaps a book needs to strike at the right time, in the right place, but of all the things I have lost, how much in shunning these authors, these stories? For the first time I find that I am not reading as a form of posturing, but reading because it is so deeply comforting to me. Escape? Sure, but I don't know where others find strength if not in a few classics.

Three Lives & Company

NEW YORK, NY

Since 1978, Three Lives & Company has offered a haven for the engaged, curious reader. Meticulously selected and beautifully presented literary fiction and nonfiction fill the shelves in this West Village bookshop, proclaimed a "pocket of civility" by the Greenwich Village Historical Society. A work in progress, Three Lives & Company is an ever-evolving respite from the usual and the expected, a place for community, discussion, and, above all, discovery in a shop celebrating the shared passion of both booksellers and customers for a good story well told.

www.threelives.com

TOBY COX, OWNER

**What's your favorite bookstore
(besides the one you work at)?**

As does every bookseller I know, whenever I travel I visit as many bookstores as I can. When I was in Los Angeles I made a friend drive me all over that sprawling metropolis to visit bookstores. When visiting family in San Francisco, usually after a lunch at Zuni, I wander up Market Street to call on the Green Arcade bookstore. An amazing collection of books that reflect the many interests of the owner, Patrick Marks, this is one bookstore I can browse in for a long time. I generally find it hard to wander new bookstores, because of the sense that I know most of what is available and what is on hand, but in the Green Arcade I am humbled by the subjects on display, the books highlighted, the energy I feel in the shop. To browse is to discover, and the inspired selection at the Green Arcade leads me on a fascinating journey, one on which I learn a great deal.

What would be book number 51 on your list?

I mentioned to a customer that I was putting together a list of my favorite fifty books for a bookseller in Saint Paul and she asked that I send it along to her. Within minutes of hitting send she wrote back with all sorts of comments, but her very first: "What about *The City of Your Final Destination,* by Peter Cameron? You love that book!" She's right. A writer with incredible grace, Cameron's novel tells a simple tale with some extraordinary characters. But my passion for that novel is that it is told with such honesty, such compassion for his characters, with such a deft touch of feeling and motivation, yet without the use of dramatics or ghosts clattering out of the closet.

TOBY'S LIST

- [ ] **Wilderness Tips,** Margaret Atwood
- [ ] **Another Country,** James Baldwin
- [ ] **The Feast of Love,** Charles Baxter
- [ ] **2666,** Roberto Bolaño
- [ ] **Mystery Ride,** Robert Boswell
- [ ] **The Children's Book,** A. S. Byatt
- [ ] **The Beans of Egypt, Maine,** Carolyn Chute
- [ ] **Disgrace,** J. M. Coetzee
- [ ] **Hero,** Frederick G. Dillen
- [ ] **The Royal Physician's Visit,** Per Olov Enquist
- [ ] **Love Medicine,** Louise Erdrich
- [ ] **The Waitress Was New,** Dominique Fabre
- [ ] **The Sound and the Fury,** William Faulkner
- [ ] **Then We Came to the End,** Joshua Ferris
- [ ] **The Good Doctor,** Damon Galgut
- [ ] **Mister Sandman,** Barbara Gowdy
- [ ] **Life and Fate,** Vasily Grossman
- [ ] **The Dream Life of Sukhanov,** Olga Grushin
- [ ] **The Great Fire,** Shirley Hazzard
- [ ] **Balcony of Europe,** Aidan Higgins

- [ ] **The Known World,** Edward P. Jones
- [ ] **Snow Country,** Yasunari Kawabata
- [ ] **Walk the Blue Fields,** Claire Keegan
- [ ] **The Conqueror,** Jan Kjærstad
- [ ] **A Thousand Years of Good Prayers,** Yiyun Li
- [ ] **The Chateau,** William Maxwell
- [ ] **By the Lake,** John McGahern
- [ ] **Cloud Atlas,** David Mitchell
- [ ] **The Ice Storm,** Rick Moody
- [ ] **In Other Rooms, Other Wonders,** Daniyal Mueenuddin
- [ ] **The Discovery of Heaven,** Harry Mulisch
- [ ] **The Wind-Up Bird Chronicle,** Haruki Murakami
- [ ] **The Things They Carried,** Tim O'Brien
- [ ] **Snow Angels,** Stewart O'Nan
- [ ] **Divisadero,** Michael Ondaatje
- [ ] **The Echo Maker,** Richard Powers
- [ ] **The Shipping News,** Annie Proulx
- [ ] **The God of Small Things,** Arundhati Roy
- [ ] **Last Night,** James Salter
- [ ] **Light Years,** James Salter
- [ ] **CivilWarLand in Bad Decline,** George Saunders
- [ ] **Lucky Us,** Joan Silber
- [ ] **Shadows on the Hudson,** Isaac Bashevis Singer

- [ ] **Crossing to Safety,** Wallace Stegner
- [ ] **The Grapes of Wrath,** John Steinbeck
- [ ] **Pereira Declares: A Testimony,** Antonio Tabucchi
- [ ] **Triomf,** Marlene van Niekerk
- [ ] **Separate Checks,** Marianne Wiggins
- [ ] **Cloudstreet,** Tim Winton
- [ ] **This Boy's Life,** Tobias Wolff

The Known World, Edward P. Jones
I'm with Dave Eggers on this one; a classic upon publication, *The Known World* is one of the Great Books of American literature.

Walk the Blue Fields, Claire Keegan
The grand Irish literary tradition continues with these remarkable short stories set in contemporary rural Ireland. Only her second story collection yet Keegan is already a master of the form and a writer to be celebrated.

The Conqueror, Jan Kjærstad
Finishing this mesmerizing Norwegian novel I thought to myself: This is why I read. Rich, morally complex, engrossing, *The Conqueror* is an enthralling read.

Unabridged Bookstore

CHICAGO, IL

Since 1980, Unabridged Bookstore has been serving the city of Chicago, in the Lake View neighborhood, to deliver all of its multifaceted book needs. They offer everything from the classics of literature to the latest historical biography, to LGBTQ studies and everything in between. Shoppers will find handwritten recommendations from staff in every section of the store. Unabridged has an award-winning children's section, as well as a sale book section featuring new handpicked publisher remainders at discounted prices.

www.unabridgedbookstore.com

STEFAN MOOREHEAD,
BUYER AND MANAGER

Who is your most trusted source for book recommendations?
When I'm trying to decide what book to read next, I trust anyone who's passionate about a book they've read. Books are both personal and universal, so if there's even the hint of a life-changing moment, or a bit of fun, I pounce on that book and want to give it every conceivable chance to do the same again and hopefully again when I can sling it back at a customer with verve and passion. This, however, is one of the pitfalls of being a bookseller: being overimbibed on fine books. There are so many to choose from, so many passionate readers, and only so many reading hours in the day. I think back to that first book that set me off on the long, winding road of constant readership, Norton Juster's *The Phantom Tollbooth,* and I know that through all the reading I've accomplished, it's a life I wish on everyone.

- ☐ **The Hitchhiker's Guide to the Galaxy,** Douglas Adams
- ☐ **The Hakawati,** Rabih Alameddine
- ☐ **The President Is a Sick Man: Wherein the Supposedly Virtuous Grover Cleveland Survives a Secret Surgery at Sea and Vilifies the Courageous Newspaperman Who Dared Expose the Truth,** Matthew Algeo
- ☐ **People are Unappealing: Even Me,** Sara Barron
- ☐ **Hold Everything Dear: Dispatches on Survival and Resistance,** John Berger
- ☐ **The Savage Detectives,** Roberto Bolaño
- ☐ **The Mystery Guest,** Grégoire Bouillier
- ☐ **American Salvage,** Bonnie Jo Campbell
- ☐ **2001: A Space Odyssey,** Arthur C. Clarke
- ☐ **Childhood's End,** Arthur C. Clarke
- ☐ **The Lunatic at Large,** J. Storer Clouston
- ☐ **A Splendid Conspiracy,** Albert Cossery
- ☐ **I Drink for a Reason,** David Cross
- ☐ **About a Mountain,** John D'Agata
- ☐ **The Brief Wondrous Life of Oscar Wao,** Junot Díaz
- ☐ **The Last Werewolf,** Glen Duncan
- ☐ **A Visit from the Goon Squad,** Jennifer Egan
- ☐ **You Shall Know Our Velocity,** Dave Eggers

- [ ] **Lunar Park,** Bret Easton Ellis
- [ ] **Visitation,** Jenny Erpenbeck
- [ ] **The Sound and the Fury,** William Faulkner
- [ ] **Another Bullshit Night in Suck City,** Nick Flynn
- [ ] **Freedom,** Jonathan Franzen
- [ ] **Memory of Fire** (trilogy), Eduardo Galeano
- [ ] **Neuromancer,** William Gibson
- [ ] **Lord of Misrule,** Jaimy Gordon
- [ ] **The Forever War,** Joe Haldeman
- [ ] **Stanley: The Impossible Life of Africa's Greatest Explorer,** Tim Jeal
- [ ] **Tree of Smoke,** Denis Johnson
- [ ] **Sometimes a Great Notion,** Ken Kesey
- [ ] **On Writing: A Memoir of the Craft,** Stephen King
- [ ] **The Ask,** Sam Lipsyte
- [ ] **Embassytown,** China Miéville
- [ ] **Cloud Atlas,** David Mitchell
- [ ] **The Thousand Autumns of Jacob de Zoet,** David Mitchell
- [ ] **The Wind-Up Bird Chronicle,** Haruki Murakami
- [ ] **The Tiger's Wife,** Téa Obreht
- [ ] **Scott Pilgrim** (series), Bryan Lee O'Malley
- [ ] **The Language Instinct: How the Mind Creates Language,** Steven Pinker

- [ ] **The Braindead Megaphone,** George Saunders

- [ ] **Bottomless Belly Button,** Dash Shaw

- [ ] **Absurdistan,** Gary Shteyngart

- [ ] **Super Sad True Love Story,** Gary Shteyngart

- [ ] **Blood Horses: Notes of a Sportswriter's Son,**
  John Jeremiah Sullivan

- [ ] **Conscience: Two Soldiers, Two Pacifists, One Family—
  A Test of Will and Faith in World War I,** Louisa Thomas

- [ ] **Blankets,** Craig Thompson

- [ ] **A Confederacy of Dunces,** John Kennedy Toole

- [ ] **The Pale King,** David Foster Wallace

- [ ] **Seeing is Forgetting the Name of the Thing One Sees:
  A Life of Contemporary Artist Robert Irwin,**
  Lawrence Weschler

- [ ] **Local,** Brian Wood

The Lunatic at Large, J. Storer Clouston
Recently republished by Paul Collins and McSweeney's, this is a novel I love to hand to people and say, "See, not so much has changed in the last hundred years. We can still laugh at ourselves until we pee our pants." Also, the book itself looks great on the shelf and calls to people to pick it up and read its delicious first lines. There is also the best bit of historical trivia connected to this book: the word *bonkers* originated from Clouston's hand.

The Sound and the Fury, William Faulkner
I picked this particular Faulkner not just because it's one of my top five favorite novels ever written, but because I relish how it challenges a reader. I want others to take the same trip with me past its shifting perspectives and unique sense of itself. I won't lie, this is a hard sell to non-Faulkner torchbearers, but the payoff is absolute and gratifying. This is an amazing example of what a novel can do.

Scott Pilgrim (series), Bryan Lee O'Malley
Graphic novels are, to some, a style to be avoided at all costs, but I love busting people's notion of what a graphic novel is with this, since there is no reason to fear in O'Malley's capable hands. This six-chapter arc has a

stellar plot, amazing characters and development, and enough genre red meat to keep even fangirls/boys happy. But it's tender and loving and schmaltzy in all of the right places. I love handing the first book to people and saying, "Just try the first one." They inevitably come back for the rest.

Breaking Down the Books (and the Bookstores)

Which book is listed most often? *The Things They Carried,* by Tim O'Brien, 6 times.

Which author is listed most often? William Faulkner, 12 times

Which author has the most books listed? William Faulkner, 6 works (*Absalom, Absalom!, As I Lay Dying, Light in August, The Sound and the Fury, The Unvanquished,* and *Short Selected Stories*). Ernest Hemingway was a close second with 5 works.

How many books are collections/anthologies? 20

How many books are poetry? 11

How many book series are listed? 5

Which book listed has the shortest title? *Bear,* by Marian Engel, *Grub,* by Elise Blackwell, and *Zoom,* by Istvan Banyai

Longest Title? *The President Is a Sick Man: Wherein the Supposedly Virtuous Grover Cleveland Survives a Secret Surgery at Sea and Vilifies the Courageous Newspaperman Who Dared Expose the Truth,* by Matthew Algeo

What is the total number of books represented? 1,194 (993 unique volumes)

How many books are recommended more than once? 144

Titles containing the word "Love": 19

Titles containing the word "Death": 6

BOOKSTORE STATISTICS:

Oldest bookstore: Sherman's Books and Stationery, 126 years

Youngest bookstore: Boswell Book Company, 3 years

Number of stores 25 years or older: 17

Number of Yoko Ono sightings: 1 (Tattered Cover Book Store)

Number of stores that have hosted presidents: 5 (Book Passage, the King's English Bookshop, Prairie Lights Books, the Regulator Bookshop, and Tattered Cover Book Store)

Bookstores President Obama visited before he became president: 4 (Book Passage, Prairie Lights Books, RiverRun Bookstore, and Tattered Cover Book Store)

Bookstores President Obama has visited since becoming president: 1 (Prairie Lights Books)

Largest store: 20,000 square feet (Tattered Cover Book Store)

Smallest store: 700 square feet (Three Lives & Company)

Largest inventory: 150,000 books (Magers and Quinn)

Smallest inventory: 6,500 titles (Three Lives & Company)

Bookstores with multiple locations: 6 (Book Passage, Carmichael's Bookstore, and Skylight Books have 2 each; Tattered Cover Book Store and Square Books have 3 each; and Sherman's Books and Stationery has 4.)

Bookstore that holds the most monthly events: Book Passage (40–50 events per month), followed closely by Tattered Cover Book Store (averages 40 events per month across its three locations)

Number of bookstores that hold Emily Dickinson look-alike contests: 1 (Fireside Books)

Bookstores with connections to Allen Ginsberg's *Howl*: 2 (At City Lights, store cofounder Lawrence Ferlinghetti and former store clerk Shig Murao were arrested for selling the book. Fireside Books held a *Howl* fiftieth anniversary celebration, which won an award from City Lights).

Number of bookstores who have mascots/pets: 6 (housing 3 dogs, 2 cats, and 2 people-size teddy bears)

Number of bookstores who used to keep bees on the roof of their shop: 1 (Maria's Bookshop)

Number of bookstores whose dog is often found napping on the floor: 1 (BookCourt)

Number of bookstores with a live tree growing inside the store: 1 (Skylight Books)

Number of bookstores with the goal of being "one of the oddest bookstores in the land": 1 (Micawbers Books)

BOOKSELLER STATISTICS:

Most veteran bookseller: Paul Yamazaki of City Lights Bookstore (42 years)

Newest to the business: Emma Straub of BookCourt (3 years)

Most voracious reader: Liberty Hardy of RiverRun Bookstore (25–35 books per month)

Number of booksellers who admit to reading more than one book at a time: 2 (Eowyn Ivey of Fireside Books and Paul Yamazaki of City Lights)

Best excuse for not reading more: "Out mowing the field." (Matt Lage of Iowa Book, who still manages an average of 6 books per month.)

Number of booksellers who are also published authors: 5

Number of booksellers who are also *New York Times* best-selling authors: 1 (Eowyn Ivey of Fireside Books)

About the ABFFE

The American Booksellers Foundation for Free Expression is the bookseller's voice in the fight against censorship. Founded by the American Booksellers Association in 1990, ABFFE's mission is to promote and protect the free exchange of ideas, particularly those contained in books, by opposing restrictions on the freedom of speech; issuing statements on significant free expression controversies; participating in legal cases involving First Amendment rights; collaborating with other groups with an interest in free speech; and providing education about the importance of free expression to booksellers, other members of the book industry, politicians, the press, and the public.

www.abffe.org

MY LIST OF MY 50 FAVORITE BOOKS

- [ ] _____
- [ ] _____
- [ ] _____
- [ ] _____
- [ ] _____
- [ ] _____
- [ ] _____
- [ ] _____
- [ ] _____
- [ ] _____
- [ ] _____
- [ ] _____
- [ ] _____
- [ ] _____
- [ ] _____
- [ ] _____
- [ ] _____
- [ ] _____

- [ ] _____
- [ ] _____
- [ ] _____
- [ ] _____
- [ ] _____
- [ ] _____
- [ ] _____
- [ ] _____
- [ ] _____
- [ ] _____
- [ ] _____
- [ ] _____
- [ ] _____
- [ ] _____
- [ ] _____
- [ ] _____
- [ ] _____
- [ ] _____
- [ ] _____
- [ ] _____

BOOKSTORES I'VE VISITED

- ☐ Book Passage
- ☐ BookCourt
- ☐ Boswell Book Company
- ☐ Carmichael's Bookstore
- ☐ City Lights
- ☐ Faulkner House Books
- ☐ Fireside Books
- ☐ Harvard Book Store
- ☐ Inkwood Books
- ☐ Iowa Book
- ☐ The King's English Bookshop
- ☐ Magers and Quinn
- ☐ Maria's Bookshop
- ☐ Micawber's Books
- ☐ Prairie Lights
- ☐ Rakestraw Books
- ☐ The Regulator Bookshop
- ☐ RiverRun Bookstore

- [ ] Sherman's Books and Stationery
- [ ] Skylight Books
- [ ] Square Books
- [ ] Subterranean Books
- [ ] Tattered Cover Book Store
- [ ] Three Lives & Company
- [ ] Unabridged Bookstore
- [ ] _____
- [ ] _____
- [ ] _____
- [ ] _____
- [ ] _____
- [ ] _____
- [ ] _____
- [ ] _____
- [ ] _____
- [ ] _____
- [ ] _____
- [ ] _____
- [ ] _____

RECOMMENDATIONS

COLOPHON

Read This! was designed at Coffee House Press,
in the historic Grain Belt Brewery's Bottling House
near downtown Minneapolis. The text is set in Garamond.
Display fonts include Bodoni and Scala Sans.

COFFEE HOUSE PRESS

MISSION

The mission of Coffee House Press is to publish exciting, vital, and enduring authors of our time; to delight and inspire readers; to contribute to the
cultural life of our community; and to enrich our literary heritage. By
building on the best traditions of publishing and the book arts, we pro-
duce books that celebrate imagination, innovation in the craft of writing,
and the many authentic voices of the American experience.

VISION

LITERATURE. We will promote literature as a vital art form, helping to
redefine its role in contemporary life. We will publish authors whose
groundbreaking work helps shape the direction of 21st-century literature. **WRITERS.** We will foster the careers of our writers by making
long-term commitments to their work, allowing them to take risks in
form and content. **READERS.** Readers of books we publish will experience new perspectives and an expanding intellectual landscape.
PUBLISHING. We will be leaders in developing a sustainable 21st-
century model of independent literary publishing, pushing the boundaries
of content, form, editing, audience development, and book technologies.

VALUES

Innovation and excellence in all activities
Diversity of people, ideas, and products
Advancing literary knowledge
Community through embracing many cultures
Ethical and highly professional management and governance practices

Good books are brewing at coffeehousepress.org

FUNDER ACKNOWLEDGMENT

Coffee House Press is an independent nonprofit literary publisher. Our books are made possible through the generous support of grants and gifts from many foundations, corporate giving programs, state and federal support, and through donations from individuals who believe in the transformational power of literature. Coffee House Press receives major operating support from the Bush Foundation, the Jerome Foundation, the McKnight Foundation, the National Endowment for the Arts, a federal agency, from Target, and in part by a grant provided by the Minnesota State Arts Board through an appropriation by the Minnesota State Legislature from the State's general fund and its arts and cultural heritage fund with money from the vote of the people of Minnesota on November 4, 2008. Coffee House also receives support from: several anonymous donors; Suzanne Allen; Elmer L. and Eleanor J. Andersen Foundation; Around Town Agency; Patricia Beithon; Bill Berkson; the E. Thomas Binger and Rebecca Rand Fund of the Minneapolis Foundation; the Patrick and Aimee Butler Family Foundation; Ruth Dayton; Dorsey & Whitney, LLP; Mary Ebert and Paul Stembler; Chris Fischbach and Katie Dublinski; Fredrikson & Byron, P.A.; Sally French; Anselm Hollo and Jane Dalrymple-Hollo; Jeffrey Hom; Carl and Heidi Horsch; Alex and Ada Katz; Stephen and Isabel Keating; the Kenneth Koch Literary Estate; Kathy and Dean Koutsky; the Lenfestey Family Foundation; Carol and Aaron Mack; Mary McDermid; Sjur Midness and Briar Andresen; the Rehael Fund of the Minneapolis Foundation; Schwegman, Lundberg & Woessner, P.A.; Kiki Smith; Jeffrey Sugerman; Patricia Tilton; the Archie D. & Bertha H. Walker Foundation; Stu Wilson and Mel Barker; the Woessner Freeman Family Foundation; Margaret and Angus Wurtele; and many other generous individual donors.

To you and our many readers across the country,
we send our thanks for your continuing support.